Unfinished Business

Ireland Today and Tomorrow

Liam de

HUTCHINSON RADIUS

LONDON   SYDNEY   AUCKLAND   JOHANNESBURG

© Liam de Paor 1990
The right of Liam de Paor to be identified as Author of this
work has been asserted by Liam de Paor in accordance with the
Copyright, Designs and Patent Act, 1988

Hutchinson Radius
An imprint of Century Hutchinson Ltd
20 Vauxhall Bridge Road, London SW1V 2SA

Century Hutchinson Australia Pty Ltd
89–91 Albion Street, Surry Hills, New
South Wales 2010, Australia

Century Hutchinson New Zealand Limited
PO Box 40–086, Glenfield, Auckland 10,
New Zealand

Century Hutchinson South Africa (Pty) Ltd,
PO Box 337, Bergvlei, 2012 South Africa

First published by Hutchinson Radius 1990

British Library Cataloguing in Publication Data
De Paor, Liam
  Unfinished business.
  1. Northern Ireland. Ethnic groups. Nationalism, history
  I. Title
  323.1'416
        ISBN 0 09 174406 7

Photoset by Speedset Ltd, Ellesmere Port
Printed and bound in Great Britain by
Mackays of Chatham Ltd, Chatham, Kent

Contents

For Cillian and Diarmaid

O most beautiful and loving brethren and children whom I begot in Christ (and whom I cannot number) – what can I do for you? I am inadequate to help either God or humans. The wickedness of the wicked has overcome us. We have been transformed into strangers. Perhaps they do not believe that we have been given the same baptism, or that we have the same God. For them it is shameful that we are Irish. As it is written: 'Have your not the one God? Why have you, one and all, abandoned your neighbour?'

St Patrick

UNFINISHED BUSINESS

Introduction

The great problems of our contemporary world are moral. Physical difficulties have been largely overcome. For the first time in its history, the human race has the technical capacity to feed, clothe and house a huge world population. This could free men, women and children everywhere from that anxiety about the necessities of life which appears to have given rise to the fears, hatreds and oppressions that have plagued humanity at least since the end of the Stone Age. But technical capacity is not enough.

We do not live by bread alone. Humans are conscious – self-conscious – and live in a world of mind, imagination, memory, aspiration and dream, as well as in a material world. We are shaped by language. We are members of communities which teach us ancestral wisdom. We belong to cultures: group artefacts through which the dead, the living and the unborn communicate and sustain one another by means of myth which directs custom. These are as necessary to us as food and warmth.

Clever as we have shown ourselves to be in manipulating the material world, we continue to fail miserably in dealing with the moral world of community and culture. This is not always through ill will, although there is plenty of ill will about. Too much of our analysis of social matters is misconceived. Consciously or unconsciously we try to deal with social events as if they were mechanical processes. The notion, for example, of atomized human individuals autonomously seeking their own limited good, provides no ground for a solid understanding of society. It leads us back to Hobbesian modes of thinking – the war of all against all – from which we should have been freed by the insights of numerous thinkers and investigators of the past century or so, as well as by the prophets and teachers of past ages. And it leads us into the company of preachers of hatred, who also hold that competition is the primary law of life. We have seen in our time, on the other hand, what can come of the contrary error, denying the autonomy and freedom of

1

the person, reducing human souls to soldier ants or worker bees, slaves of the hive.

It is surely a combination of misguided theory on the one hand and deliberate malice on the other that has made our twentieth century – when an unprecedented liberation was possible – a time, instead, of mass murder, famine, war and torture, and of a general darkening of the mind. We have perhaps been saved so far from a Third World War by the fear shared by the great powers, fear of their own apocalyptic nuclear weapons and of what the strategic planners have called 'Mutually Assured Destruction'. But there have been many smaller wars since 1945, and, in a number of places in the world, conflicts sustained by fear, hatred and despair, which appear to be without possibility of resolution.

The conflict in Northern Ireland which first came to the attention of the world at large in the late 1960s, is not one of the greatest or the worst of these. But it has continued, with undiminished bitterness, if with somewhat diminished violence, for twenty years. It is often cited as an example of the intractable problems which we have inherited from less enlightened ages – the assumption being that our world, by and large, is run by reasonable and moderate people but that here and there, as in Belfast, there are unreasonable and immoderate people, and that it is very difficult for even the most enlightened rulers to cope with them. The assumption calls for examination.

This short book is largely concerned with that conflict, not so much in its origins as in its possible outcome. The historical background of the events in Ulster has by now been thoroughly explored by many writers. I wrote about it myself, in 1969, when the current trouble had barely begun (*Divided Ulster*, 1970), and have subsequently, in many briefer pieces, commented on it: some parts of those comments are incorporated here. It is, of course, impossible to discuss the problem usefully without reference to its history. The elaborately painted gable ends in Belfast, Derry, Armagh, Portadown and other Ulster towns – the demotic expressions of a society engaged in conflict – enjoin us to 'Remember 1690!' or to cherish the memory of Tone, Emmet, Pearse and (now receding into history) Bobby Sands. But what is proposed here is rather to take due note of the past for the light it

2

may shed on the present, and to offer suggestions for the future.

Northern Ireland is part of Ireland, as it is also part of the United Kingdom of Great Britain and Northern Ireland. The discussion has to be about the two parts of Ireland in relation to Great Britain. It is an argument stated, I hope and intend, with full respect for the candid opinions of others.

It seems to me that the Ulster conflict is, by comparison with some other disputes in the world, a muted one and that it is possible to envisage a reasonably acceptable end to it. It is necessary to begin by painting a quite gloomy picture of Ireland, North and South, at the present moment; but this is not a pessimistic book. On the contrary, it will be argued that the problems are soluble and that all of Ireland, north and south, can enjoy in the future both tranquility and modest prosperity such as have been too long absent in the past.

This does, however, require a compromise; and compromises over differences in national identity and over such matters as the distinction between a republic and a monarchy are not easy. But Ireland, a victim country, has long had an enforced understanding of the need to make daily compromises. This can be done in the present as it was done in the past.

Two solutions to the Ulster problem, frequently advocated, are out of the question. They are simply not feasible in the immediate future. One, favoured by many Protestants, is full integration into the United Kingdom and the replacement of Northern Ireland politics by British politics, with the British Conservative, Labour and other parties contesting elections in Ulster. This is a pipe dream. The British do not want it and the nationalists would prevent it. The other is Irish reunification. The loyalists would resist it and make it unworkable, and few people in the South have the stomach – or even the desire – to force it through against such opposition.

This leaves the local, Northern Ireland, solution, which must in the long run involve some form of autonomy. And the more autonomy the better. Faced with the whole responsibility, nationalists and unionists would certainly work out between them a way to run the province as an independent entity, all the more so if they had the good will and cooperation of the Dublin and London governments.

What is argued here, in other words, is that in the long run we should aim at having three states rather than two in the British Isles (more than three if the Scots and Welsh feel so disposed); that Northern Ireland should be autonomous, within the constraints of the European Community and perhaps within the constraints of the British Commonwealth; but that it should have special legally defined relationships with both the Republic and the United Kingdom.

We have to accept the truth that within the island of Ireland we have at least two histories, not one; that we must deal with complexity, not simplicity. If we do accept this, we can proceed – on ordinary (and in fact widely accepted) principles of fair dealing and civil and religious rights and liberties – to make an island in amity and justice.

Such an outcome, however, does not depend on the peoples of Ireland and Britain alone, but on a more general awakening to the need for a better world than the one we have and to the possibility of its achievement.

1

One Nation or Two?

'A Nation is a group of persons united by a common error about their ancestry and a common dislike of their neighbours.' So wrote Karl W. Deutsch, opening his book, *Nationalism and its Alternatives*, and quoting what he described as a 'rueful European saying'.

Rueful or cynical, the saying has something to it. At least it makes the point that a nation is not a datum like a mountain, or a lake, or an island. It is an artefact, a construct of human minds. And it is an essentially cultural artefact, and an abstract one, which emphasizes ideas, beliefs and traditions held in common by one group of people as distinct from other groups. It is, in other words, both inclusive and exclusive. The snag is that the 'rueful European saying' could almost equally well apply to a parish or a family.

In fact, what is significant about a nation is that it unites a number of population groups, over an extended area. What holds them together is not necessarily a common dislike of their neighbours, but a sense of common difference from them. They may believe this or that about their ancestors, but among themselves they are aware of two things: a high level of mutual understanding (this usually, but not always, implies a common language) and a high level of interdependence.

Nations are constructs. They are formed by history. Usually they have been formed partly by political processes, through which the more or less universal mutual hostility between neighbouring villages or tribes is subsumed in wider allegiances, in the transference of hostility to more remote 'foreigners', and in the sense of fates being bound together. Such a process is virtually impossible without some sort of centralized organization. This need not be political in the beginning (it may be cultural or religious) but the creation of a state from an earlier tribalism appears to be a common mode of nation building.

The formation of nations has been particularly a feature of European history, and most of the European nations are now about a thousand years old, and mature in their nationhood. The Irish nation is older. Fifteen hundred years ago, when our records are about beginning, it is fairly clear that the people of Ireland, although politically they were divided into many small and more or less autonomous chiefdoms, acknowledged that they belonged to a single nation. It was coterminous with the island, and it had a name (*Ériu*) which was not a group or population name. It is this, perhaps, that has made people in Ireland sometimes forget that the nation is an artefact. It is often treated as if it were a fact of nature. Unlike the other European nations it has had, for fifteen hundred years, in the common understanding, a firm and clearly defined location. So there has been something of a tendency to argue as if geography in itself creates and defines the nation. It is not really possible to think in this way about, say, Germany, or Poland, or Bohemia. With such countries one is immediately driven to definitions in human, historical and cultural terms.

One of the many cross-purposes in our current confusion arises from this. Ulster unionists nowadays usually prefer to define their polity in such human, cultural and historical terms: they are a people historically derived from a migration of English and Scottish colonists who settled in Ireland. This no doubt is an over-simplification, but it expresses well enough for present purposes the sense they have of themselves – including the ambiguities that attach to the term 'British'. Yet, most of the unionists think of themselves – 'non-politically' – as Irish. Politically, they think of themselves, under various labels, as subjects of the British Queen and citizens of the United Kingdom, and their sense of Irishness would seem to have weakened in the past century under the pressure of political events. Few of them now, although 'Irish', would describe themselves as members of the 'Irish nation'.

A little over a hundred years ago, the unity of Ireland as a nation was fairly generally accepted, although Ulster was known to have a character quite different from the other provinces. But throughout the eighteenth century Ireland had been a political unit, a distinct Kingdom, with its own parliament of lords and commons, and it was as a unit that it had entered the Union with Britain in 1801. The people who inhabited the island differed among themselves on many issues but shared history, culture, outlook, and, at that date, 'the common name of Irish'. Admittedly, this definition was open to question and was being questioned by some, because of the profound differences in political aspiration that were apparent. The great divide was fully exposed as it opened wide with the first Home Rule Bill, of 1886.

It has been the common experience that nations, in modern European history at least, have tended or aspired to organize themselves as states. The 'nation-states', however, which were the characteristic political formations of post-medieval Europe, were usually to a greater or less degree multi-national. France, Spain and the United Kingdom are examples. As a result, 'nationalism' is an ambiguous term. It may refer to the aggrandizing or super-nationalism of the nation-states. Or it may refer to the reactive nationalism of the submerged nationalities like the Basques, the Bretons or (before 1914) the Czechs and the Poles.

The two are frequently in conflict. Even where they are not, there are often subtle distinctions. In Britain, where there exist (fairly weak) Scottish and Welsh nationalisms, there is also a British super-nationalism, whose ethos is maintained through the universities and schools and through the media of communication, and is often extravagant in its manifestations (as in the Falklands war). But there is also an English nationalism (*de haut en bas*). In current English usage, for example, upper- and upper-middle-class English people still prefer, whether in writing or in speech, to use the word 'English' when referring to national affairs, affirming the reality they feel in their bones: that there is a national hierarchy within the United Kingdom in which not just the English, but the southern English, are the top dogs. Such terms as 'British', 'Briton' and 'Britain' occur more commonly in the vocabularies of those who address the lower-middle class and the working class or in the language of subordinate peoples such as Scots, Welsh, Mersey-siders and Tynesiders. The word 'British' develops other nuances and shades of meaning in Ireland. The geographical expression 'the British Isles', for example, is widely disliked because it recalls the *political* memories of an unwanted Union. Great Britain is one island, Ireland another. No adequate substitute expression is available, however. The commonly used 'these islands' is obviously limited in its applicability and has no meaning when the speaker is in Canada or China.

But for Ulster loyalists to describe themselves as 'British' – and they often do – is to make rather more of a political than a 'national' or geographical statement. They are declaring adherence to a political system and a political arrangement. Since the Union first became an issue, however, the loyalists of Ulster have been searching sporadically for a 'national', as distinct from merely constitutional, identity. So we find the term 'Scotch-Irish' being applied early in the nineteenth century to the descendants of Ulster Protestant (mainly Presbyterian) settlers who migrated in the eighteenth century from Ulster to North America. The expression was retrospective (the settlers were 'Irish' when they came) but it rose naturally enough from the eighteenth-century practice of enumerating populations in Ulster with the distinctions 'Scotch', 'English' and 'Irish', as designations of origin. In the nineteenth century, when very large numbers of Irish Catholics began to cross the Atlantic, it was felt necessary to distinguish from them the posterity of those Protestants who had come over from the North of Ireland in an earlier time.

Later in the nineteenth century, at the time of the great Home Rule controversy, unionist ideologues invented a hybrid nationality and wrote in terms of high praise of a racial and national type whom they called 'the Ulster Scot'. This concept has been somewhat refined in recent years in an Ulster nationalist ideology sponsored by the UDA and formulated largely by Mr Ian Adamson. In this, history has been revised to suggest that the original folk of Ulster – there before the advent of the 'Celts' – was a common stock that lived on both sides of the North Channel, in Scotland as well as in the North of Ireland. These were the Picts of Scottish proto-history, a people sufficiently obscure to lend themselves to such manipulation. They are usually referred to, however, by a name used in early Ireland both for inhabitants of Scotland and for people living in east Ulster, and are called *Cruthin*. This brings us, by a roundabout way, back to 'Britons' and 'British'; for the word *Cruthin* is related to the words *Pretani* and *Brittani* that we find in early writings describing the inhabitants of Britain.

8

Not all Ulster unionists are affected by stirrings of Ulster nationalism; but many are, since they find a need to react not merely against the pretensions of Irish anti-Partitionist republicans and others but also against English governmental decisions that are seen as insensitive to Ulster feeling or neglectful of Ulster interests.

Nationalism, at any rate, is a marked feature of comparatively recent history and is still probably the most powerful political force in the world. It is intimately associated with rapid growth in the power and functions of the state. The Irish State, the Republic of Ireland, came into being as a result of nationalism. It was created to serve the nation by protecting it from various forms of external exploitation and by promoting the national aspirations, aspirations which were perhaps ill defined.

There are still people in Ireland who can remember the time when the Union flag flew over Dublin Castle. But they are of the most senior generation and form a tiny minority of the Irish population. More than half the population, on the other hand, can't remember a time when there was no Irish television service. That tiny minority and that majority have had very different experiences of their country. The concepts of the Irish nation possessed by the two groups are also very different. At the beginning of this century nationalism appeared to be natural and normal. It was respectable, intellectually, socially and politically. Nations were as self-evident as races. Each nation, like each race, had its distinctive characteristics, which could be readily recognized and readily stereotyped. It is a lost world. A glance through the pages of *Punch* – especially the full-page political cartoons – for the years just before the Great War, reveals a remarkable simplicity of outlook at the time, in which nations were as autonomous and identifiable as persons.

It is no longer so. The racial and other presuppositions are no longer intellectually respectable, nor, in social and political life, can they be blatantly acknowledged. Nationalism in Britain, in the United States, in France, is still a very powerful force, but it is very differently expressed, with different images. And the young Dublin person today is unlikely to think of the German, for example, as a square-headed, crop-skulled, spike-moustached, thick-spectacled, militaristic gluttonous sausage-eating dachshund-fancier; but as Hans or Helga, met in a disco in Baggot Street or Hamburg, sharing the same culture of music, sport, film, literature, even politics. For, almost unnoticed, real politics today has detached itself from nations and states to a considerable extent. The politics which is the proper business of every citizen, that which is concerned with the ordering of the public good, the politics of Aristotle, addresses itself to questions that concern the physical, psychological and moral well-being of all of us. Some, it is true, still cling to the nation as the source of well-being, the nurturer and guardian, the 'us' against the alien 'them' (this is most notable in the United States of America). But many rather find their comfort in communities of age, cohort or class.

We are concerned about peace and war. We are concerned about food, shelter, air, water, decency, amenity. We are concerned at the grim culture of unemployment and alienation that is created by the application of eighteenth- and nineteenth-century economic principles and prejudices in late-twentieth-century conditions. But all of these questions seem now to extend outside and beyond nations. The nations are still real; but the reality has changed much in the modern world. They are real because, so far, and at present, they are the available models for supplying at least two important but intangible necessities of our being. One is the sense of community, of the neighbouring presence of help in time of need, of understanding in time of distress. The other is to belong to a culture, which humanity needs as it needs the air it breathes. We must, of the nature of our species, locate ourselves in a present between past and future; we must communicate with other articulate minds; we must know who we are and what we are; we must believe in whatever we believe in; we must know a myriad rules of behaviour – how to walk on a crowded footpath; how to address a cat; how to eat peas; how to laugh at a joke; how to see an Impressionist painting; how to read a computer print-out.

The nation, in the modern world at least, has served as one of the chief vessels for culture. This may be changing now, although change is slow. Entropy appears to be the current rule in culture, as more and more parts of the world become more and more like every other part. Perhaps the appearance of this tendency to uniformity is deceptive. If not, it is paradoxical; for life is the reversal of entropy.

And, so far at any rate, cultural differences not only exist: they are strongly felt.

The federal state of Canada is, in terms of land area, the second largest in the world (after the Soviet Union). In terms of population, it is half the size of Great Britain. Nine-tenths of its population live within a hundred miles of the United States border, and about half of these are densely distributed towards the eastern seaboard. It is a highly pluralistic country, with people drawn from almost all sections of the human race, including an already highly varied population of native Americans – Inuits and Amerindians. There is a major divide between the Francophones, powerfully based in Quebec but quite strong in some other provinces, and the Anglophones who dominate most of the vast country. The divide gives rise to a forceful separatist tendency and political programme. The dominant culture is somewhat weakened by being one side of a triangle, of which the other two sides are the United Kingdom and the United States. But Canada hangs together. This is a country sufficiently conscious of its nationality, still sufficiently possessed of that mysterious silent acknowledgment of common history, common purpose, common allegiance, common interest, that makes a nation.

It is a good perspective from which to look at Irish nationality. Ireland, taking north and south together, is small and comparatively homogeneous; all parts of the island share, fairly fully, in the dominant common culture of the Western world, while those aspects and elements of culture which are distinctively Irish are for the most part shared also, throughout the island. By all such tests, Ireland as whole is a very good example of what is meant by a nation. But the model breaks down immediately when we apply the crucial test of the 'acknowledgment of common history, common purpose, common allegiance, common interest'. Indeed it breaks down very badly. Yet that acknowledgment would be near-unanimous if we applied the test within the twenty-six-county State. And within the territory of that State the homogeneity is quite remarkable by modern standards. Is the twenty-six-county State a nation then? Its people have never thought of this large part of Ireland as a nation. The State, significantly, has no satisfactory formal name, since it has insisted on building into the names by which it calls itself

11

('Ireland', and 'The Republic of Ireland') a claim to the whole island.

Is Northern Ireland a nation? The model breaks down more seriously there. Even the cultural homogeneity breaks down somewhat, because of the division in Christian belief and practice (although both Protestantism and Catholicism in Ulster are distinctively 'Irish' in their manifestations). Is it part of the English, the Scottish or the British nation? Of the British nation for certain purposes; but the British don't really think of it that way and are at pains to distance themselves in many respects from that part of the United Kingdom which is Irish, while a large part of the Northern Irish population rejects the British label. On the other hand, the larger part has a powerful sense of communal separateness.

The sense of separateness does not translate into a full nationalism. Ulster unionists – many of them – still have a sense of being colonials. They represent, on the island of Ireland, something from elsewhere. But elsewhere is elsewhere. Their soil is Irish. Their heritage is British. Since the time when their forebears crossed the Channel to Ireland, those whose soil remains British have steadily diverged from them in political thought and outlook. Ulster people cherish memories that have been discarded by the people of Britain and have acquired memories that have little or nothing to do with the people of Britain. They have inherited Ireland as well as 'the English Constitution'.

St Patrick, as patron saint of the whole island, has contrived to adapt himself very well to the requirements of his people. Protestant or Catholic according to how you read him, sometimes singular, sometimes dual, sometimes appearing not to be there at all. Is Ireland a nation? Yes and no. It depends on what you mean by 'nation'.

And further questions must be asked. Does it matter whether Ireland is or is not a nation? And what bearing has it, or should it have, on politics? Obviously, in practice it has a serious effect on politics. A bloody conflict is concerned largely with the question of nationality. Where the existence of the nation is unquestioned, statehood may or may not be won for it through war or politics. But the conflict certainly cannot answer the question, which is highly abstract.

There are two states in the island, one of them sovereign and independent – whatever in practice that may mean in the context of the current world economy, not to speak of the European Community – and the other a province of the United Kingdom, subordinate to the Westminster Parliament and to the unwritten and unpredictable British Constitution. The existence of the two states gives expression to two opposed systems of political allegiance. In practice, for most matters that do not concern the central opposition between them, the two systems are very similar – even when it comes to politics. Both, for example, practise ordinary western parliamentary democracy in forms derived from the British model. Both are English-speaking and in ten thousand aspects and practices of everyday life are very much alike.

There is, of course, one significant contrast, which matches the contrast in political allegiances sufficiently closely to reinforce it tremendously. It is the religious divide, a divide, for this particular purpose, between Irish Roman Catholicism and the rest of Irish Christianity. In the Republic something like 93 per cent of the population are Roman Catholic, if not in active faith and practice at least in family background, while almost all the rest might similarly be lumped together under the heading 'Protestant'. In Northern Ireland the division is something more like 40 per cent to 60 per cent, with Protestants in the majority. In this simple division, which of course is a very crude one, atheism and agnosticism do not count (one is reckoned as a Catholic atheist or a Protestant atheist). The equation of this religious divide with the fundamental political divide is, however, just too crude. There are very many exceptions of various kinds to be made.

There is a significant section of the population, both south and north of the Border, which tends to be, as it were, nationally (as well as sometimes religiously) agnostic. Its inclination is to support, not the aims or aspirations of the present bloody antagonisms, but simply the present structures of order and law, such as they are. Such people are well represented, for example, among the membership of the Alliance Party in Northern Ireland and in the Progressive Democratic Party, as well as in sections of the Fine Gael and other parties, in the Republic. For them, nations have no great relevance to daily life, whose comfort is maintained by acquiescence in the political and economic values of the Western world as a whole; while nationalism is an irrational force that threatens the order within which they live. But, rational or irrational, conflicting nationalisms are at issue in Northern Ireland. It may be – as will be argued here – that there is much more at issue. But the case must begin with the national question.

On the 'Green' extreme of one side are those who give their allegiance to what has been described as the 'historic Irish nation'. On the extreme of the other, 'Orange', side, allegiance is given to 'the British Constitution' (more accurately called by Bagehot 'the English Constitution'). Essentially, both allegiances are to myths; and the myths have this in common: that they make an appeal to a much longer history than is really warranted by the facts. On the Green side, for example, we have the Irish nation, independent until the twelfth century, with a rich civilization of its own; invaded then by the Normans from across the Channel, and subsequently struggling century after century against English conquest, suffering defeat after defeat but never giving up. Drastic methods were attempted to subdue Ireland: colonists were brought over and 'planted' on stolen lands; tremendous efforts were made to stamp out the Roman Catholic faith to which the Irish remained faithful; economic discrimination and neglect led to the Great Famine and mass emigration. This is myth: a rearrangement of facts mingled with fancies to produce a framework for the Green ideology and outlook.

The Orange myth does not go quite so far back: the Reformation is its real starting point – the point of liberation of mind and conscience from the tyranny of priestcraft and superstition; but, so far as the Irish part of the story is concerned, the starting point is the Irish Book of Exodus – the Plantation of Ulster, the establishment of religion and liberty in the midst of barbarism, the creation of a garden in the desert; the sufferings of the elect in the Catholic uprising of 1641 when the horrors of the Inquisition were re-enacted in the farmsteads of the planters; the great struggle for civil and ecclesiastical liberty which culminated in the Glorious Revolution of 1688 and was defended against absolutism and popery at Londonderry, Enniskillen, the Boyne and Aughrim; and, in more recent times, the defence of the Union, in arms where necessary, and the continued maintenance of the civil and religious liberties which have ever been under constant threat.

There may not be many people nowadays who would consciously hold and express either myth in such simple terms (although there are some; and history lessons on these lines can be found in the pages of partisan publications of the past twenty years). But they both appeal to a long history. The appeal is not wholly justified. While it is always helpful to look to the past – even far into the past – in order to understand institutions and events, this is not the same as following present institutions back and back as if they were solid immutable bodies floating down the centuries. Change is the law of time and therefore of history. But we all long for permanence, not change, and we react to the mutability of reality either with sentimental nostalgia or, sometimes, with insistence on the immutability of our own particular Rock of Ages, whatever it may be.

This is to describe, summarily, the extremes, in particular as they are to be found in Northern Ireland. Turning South, where the Green myth has its adherents in fair numbers, we may measure their commitment to it in terms of hot, tepid, or cold – and will find a predominance of tepid and cold. For the Republic, it must be remembered, the national question was answered at the end of the turbulent first quarter of the twentieth century – except that Partition left for the nation a large amount of unfinished business to be attended to some day. Nationalism became irredentism, simmering away until those exciting days at the end of the 1960s when rebellion raised the green flag again in the North. Then people, in Dublin, Cork, Kerry or Connemara, who were not troubled in their own daily lives by questions of nationality, found suddenly that the myth could confront them with difficult choices.

The choices facing the people of the Republic are the nub of the Irish national question today, even though the question has been posed by people in the North. The Northern uprising called the bluff of the South's political rhetoric. It summoned up the ghost of Patrick Pearse, who had cut across the long, slow and tedious process of parliamentary action to achieve Home Rule, and had led the bloody uprising of Easter, 1916. Pearse, the romantically heroic figure who had displaced the prosaic John Redmond in the effort to achieve Irish independence, was the political patron saint of the Irish State in the middle decades of the century.

In the Republic, a political outlook resembling the Redmondism of the early part of the century has come into fashion again in recent years. 'Redmondism' was simply the colouring Irish nationalist parliamentary politics took on in the decades after the fall of Parnell. Like many configurations in real, as distinct from theoretical, politics, it is comparatively easy to recognize but comparatively difficult to define.

A small group of politicians and writers gave this colouring to the period after the mending of the Parnell split – including, of course, John Redmond himself, the leader of the parliamentary party.* Redmondism was quite different in its character from Parnellism (although Redmond had been the most steadfastly loyal of Parnell's lieutenants at the time of the split), and it came to have somewhat different objectives. It lacked that intensity of focus, that concentration of energy in the lonely apex where the Leader fitfully functioned, enigmatic and aloof and driven by furies. Parnell was like a creation of Novalis or Shelley. Redmond was comfortably a contemporary of Asquith and Taft, and could have been invented by Galsworthy.

Apart from the personal, there was another main difference. Redmondism was marked by an acceptance of what was currently taken to be the real world. It was built on accommodation to British power and interests, and on the recognition of the permanence of that modern order that was dominated by such institutions as the British Empire. Redmondism shifted the nationalist emphasis from separatism *per se* and sought rather a place for Ireland within the imperial scheme. It was compatible with certain kinds of imperialism and could fit into that spectrum of opinion that formed the grand debate on the future of the Empire which, at one level of political activity, occupied the attention of the time. This was rational and comprehensible. It conformed to one of the main traditions of Irish politics and was probably representative of the

*John Redmond (1856–1918), Parnell's successor as leader of the Irish Nationalist Party from 1890. He secured the introduction of a Home Rule Bill which was passed on the eve of the First World War but suspended for its duration. Redmond was eclipsed by the rise of Sein Féin after the 1916 Rising.

majority view of the inhabitants of Ireland at most periods in modern times. While this tradition quite frequently employed the high-flown rhetoric of romantic nationalism, at heart it was practical and pragmatic.

In contrast, conspiratorial revolutionary movements in Ireland were, to a large extent, nationalist only as a secondary development. In origin they have often been local and *ad hoc*, addressing grievances arising more from tithe and rent and the like than from more abstract injustices. But they were widespread, registering a comprehensive belief that the ordering of affairs, parish by parish throughout the country, was unjust, and developing this belief into an ideology. And the man who was hanged for some bloody deed on behalf of the people spoke more directly to their hearts than the advocate who enjoyed a comfortable living while submitting petitions for them. But only very rarely could revolutionaries take command of these resentments on a nation-wide scale. Mostly, they had to defer to the less extreme tradition of petitioning, of forming committees, of electing people to the British parliament and of patient rationality, which normally exercised such command.

Addressing the great meeting of 31 March 1912 in support of the third Home Rule Bill, Patrick Pearse said (I translate from his Irish):

There are some of us willing to accept the sovereignty of the King of England so long as we have freedom in our own territory; that is, that foreigners should not interfere in matters that concern the Irish only . . . There are others of us who never bowed head or bent knee to the King of England and who never will. As everyone knows, I belong to this second group. But it seems to me that it would be equivalent to treachery to my people on the day of battle not to respond to today's rallying call; since it is clear to me that the Bill being proposed today will be in Irish interests, and that the Irish will be stronger for the fight with it than without it. . . . Let us unite and win a good Bill from the foreigners. I think we can win a good Bill from them if we summon up enough courage. And if we are deceived in this instance, there are those in Ireland, and I am one of them, who will advise the Irish never again to have relations or counsel with the foreigners, but to answer them with the strong arm and the sword's edge. Let the foreigners understand that if we are tricked again it will be red bloody war in Ireland.

Pearse's was a minority voice. It was Redmond's day. Pearse's was not only a minority voice, but one which most people would not have understood. The 'foreigners' (*Gaill*) he referred to were those who had been ruling Ireland for centuries, and they would certainly not have understood him in 1912. In 1920–21, when the 'red bloody war' was a reality, one of the things which most perplexed the British government was that the Irish took seriously, as a matter of politics in the real world, their claim to separate nationhood.

Redmond's failure two years later, in 1914, when Home Rule was passed but promptly suspended, with unionism in arms against it, gave the minority view its chance. The long tedium of the committee rooms, it was now accepted in Ireland, led only to the kind of betrayal Pearse had in mind: 'three things not to trust: the heels of a horse, the horns of a bull, the word of an Englishman.' Redmond's victory in parliament was undone by Carson's rebellion in arms. The unionists had proved Pearse's point: what the British, or any other imperial power for that matter, responded to in the long run was not argument but force.

And such was the turn of events that when Irish independence came about at last it was not under the auspices of the tradition that had represented the broad consensus for more than a hundred years but through the leadership of small revolutionary groups. Their tradition provided the public philosophy of the new State. Just because this happened, Redmondism seemed discredited. There was more to it than that. A self-respecting nation achieved its own independence. It did not obtain it by gift of its conqueror. Redmond was the spurned petitioner. Self-reliance – Sinn Féin – had won the day. In the twenties, thirties and forties, Irish people felt that they themselves had achieved something, not by supplication but by assertion. The declaration of the Republic in 1948 gave expression to a sense of confident self-esteem.

But the Redmondite tradition has re-emerged, partly, no doubt, because it was the majority tradition and was overwhelmingly the tradition of the classes with a material stake in the country, the professional people and those of some property, to whom revolutionary change at most times had little to offer; whose grievances did not wholly outweigh the many benefits they enjoyed under the *ancien régime*. Their opinions were muted for many decades, but they continued to be held, and even quietly expressed. In the bloody struggle from 1919 to 1921, there was little scope for constitutional agitation. The government of the Irish Free State from 1922 to 1932, although it had emerged from the 'physical force' movement ('men of violence' is the expression today) was seen as moderate in comparison with the unreconstructed republican opposition – in spite of its ruthless execution of prisoners without charge or trial. The Redmondite tradition rallied to it. The membership of the Cumann na nGaedheal succession to Sinn Féin was diluted with survivors of the old parliamentary party.*

But with the electoral victory of Fianna Fáil in 1932, the alternative, radical, nationalist tradition seemed for a while to have moved securely into command of majority opinion. The appearance was deceptive. Radicalism soon faded. The renewal of violent conflict in Ireland after the events of 1968–69 brought about some realignment of political forces throughout the island and a re-assessment of political reality in which many have returned to Redmondite values, while others, who always retained those values, have found themselves justified.

In short, radical and violent nationalism, by a conjunction of events (including in particular the overwhelmingly violent events of the Great War), occupied centre stage in Ireland for a short period in the early part of the century. In most of the island, since then, it has become marginal again, and a quite different political tradition has resumed the centre. But the failure of the British political experiment of Northern Ireland has returned violent radical nationalism to centre stage again – within Northern Ireland, but not in the Republic. An old failure is re-enacted. It is a failure of British government.

---

*The Nationalist Party was often referred to as the 'parlimentary' party to distinguish it from the republican or 'physical force' tradition.

2

Conflict and the Union

Violence is shocking. It needs an elaborate framework of social approval – inculcations of the 'military virtues' at school and in public ceremonies; rituals with uniforms and flags; State propaganda; the casting of some alien community in the role of bogey – to make it acceptable, and even then the violence should preferably take place at a distance, and under the control of conventions and rules.

Although less dangerous, less destructive, less callous, less unsparing of the innocent than regular modern war, terrorism is more frightening. It is unpredictable. It is not under approved control. It spills the blood on our streets; not in distant places. '*We are not like that*', said Mrs Thatcher after the attempt to assassinate her and other members of her government by means of the bomb in their Brighton hotel in 1984. She distinguished herself and civilized people in general from those who had just tried to murder her. The sailors of the *General Belgrano* might not agree. But Mrs Thatcher was right, not just hypocritical. There is a real and important difference. To live cheek-by-jowl, or face-to-face, with violence is to be on the steep downhill road to barbarism. To distance oneself from one's own violence may be to take the first step towards its renunciation altogether. Redmondism and neo-Redmondism, in at least part of their intention, represent an attempt at this civilized distancing. But there is a problem. Not everyone, not every cause, can command an army to fight at a distance away from hearth and home.

Violence was endemic in Ireland throughout the nineteenth century, induced by misery, discontent and frustration. Many of those who wished for an orderly autonomous Irish society feared and eschewed such violence. Parnell, however, in his under-

20

standing of the power he faced in England, while staying himself within the rule of law, drew upon the potential of violence at his back, skilfully and effectively, rather as Paisley does today.

But Redmond and his followers did not. Their approach was rather to appeal to Britain's interest in having Ireland as a free partner; to tolerate rather than oppose the socially sanctioned violence of imperial England, hoping to help redirect it into fights for 'just' causes. Redmond, it is true, understood Parnell's method, and spoke of emulating it in a speech at Maryborough in October, 1901:

My guiding principle in public life is perfectly simple. I have no faith, and never had, in any English political party. I have no faith, and never had, in English benevolence towards Ireland. I have no faith, and never had, in the possibility of any class of our population getting justice in the smallest particular for mere reason or argument or persuasion. No! We have never got anything, from the days of O'Connell down to today, without labour or suffering or sacrifice on our part, or without making a movement dangerous and menacing towards England.

The failure of the Redmondites came, indeed, when they discovered that the government they bargained with had, when it came to it, more respect for non-constitutional violence than for their reasonings.

Part of the basis for the revival of their outlook, chiefly in the twenty-six rather than in the six counties, is that the course of revolutionary conspiracy has turned back towards local and *ad hoc* issues. We have seen, over the two decades of current bloody conflict, the armed Irish groups move away from a primary concern with all-Ireland issues and aspirations towards an increasingly bewildering and private tangle of local factions and vendettas. But British force remains unified, simple in its purpose, comprehensible. The old habit of petitioning that force reasserted itself.

There are other considerations, which must be discussed later. The Home Rule province, carved out of Ulster by gerrymander, which the British set up in 1920, collapsed at the end of the 1960s. That collapse was not the result of Dublin policy. Although all parties in the twenty-six-county State (the Irish Free State of 1922–1937, the nameless entity of 1937–1948, and the Republic of 1948) had nationalist programmes and rejected Partition as a permanent solution to Irish divisions, none, in or out of government, had done anything effective about it.

The collapse of the Northern Ireland system was due to stresses set up as a result of internal contradictions. The Home Rule arrangement, created for the mangled province by the Government of Ireland Act, 1920, established a dual government. Westminster, to whose House of Commons Northern Ireland returned twelve members in general elections, retained all ultimate power and control, but the governance of internal affairs (with some exceptions) was devolved on to a local parliament (which built itself a home at Stormont in east Belfast) from whose fifty-two-member house of commons and twenty-six-member senate a ministry was chosen after Northern Ireland elections. Here the Unionist Party held permanent sway, election after election, for more than half a century, persuading the remarkably diverse Protestants of the six counties, of all classes and of all political outlooks, that they must hang together and create a one-party state. Any splitting of the vote would let in the Catholic nationalists, who would hand over all of Protestant Ulster to be governed from Dublin. Some Catholics too, who were happy enough with their lot, voted Unionist. A large part of the Catholic population gave up, rarely finding anyone to vote for in general elections.

Westminster did not exercise its powers of intervention, but left the Unionists to it, so long as things remained reasonably quiet. The Unionist Party, partly through its exercise of political power and patronage at provincial level, partly through its intimate connections with the wholly Protestant Orange Order at local level, proceeded to form a two-tier society in which Protestants, of every social, economic and political colour, enjoyed privileges (sometimes real, sometimes purely notional) which were denied to Catholics. This was not in tune with the way things had developed and were developing in Britain (although it matched well enough the Britain of an earlier time), nor was the electoral history of Northern Ireland under Stormont normal for a Western democracy. It was indeed the enforced measures of equalization that began to be employed in post-war Northern Ireland through the application there of the new British social services that brought the strains in the society to breaking point.

Not a nationalist, but a civil rights campaign led to the collapse. However, that statement, although not untrue, begs a question. Was the civil rights campaign, as it would seem in retrospect, serving the nationalist cause? It is arguable that, on the contrary, Irish nationalism throughout its modern history since the seventeenth century, has been serving a civil rights cause. And this brings us to the central question of the tangled connections of politics and religion in modern Ireland.

Only a minority of Irish nationalists before the events of 1912–1922 aimed at setting up a separate sovereign Irish State. The main engine of Irish nationalism was grievance demanding redress. And grievance, since the sixteenth century, has been closely related to the religious divide which opened then. Initially, its political manifestations were among the landowning and ruling classes. In the military and political conflicts that divided those classes in Britain and Ireland in the seventeenth century, the older land-owners in Ireland (both members of the old Gaelic families and 'Old English' descendants of medieval colonists and settlers), remained Catholic, supported the Stuarts and eventually lost their lands by confiscation. When the 'Old Irish' and the 'Old English' came together and made common cause in the middle of the century (in spite of a long history of mutual hostilities) they set up a pseudo-parliament, the Catholic Confederation, at Kilkenny, and attempted to negotiate with Charles I, through his Deputy, for a constitution for a Catholic Kingdom of Ireland. Meanwhile, a large colony of Calvinist Scots and Episcopalian English had been planted in Ulster; and the King had a Protestant parliament in Dublin, which, after his defeat by the English Parliament, joined the Cromwellian republic.

The Catholic Jacobites, after their final defeat at the end of the century, were extirpated. A new colonial landownership was established in Ireland, rewarded with the confiscated lands by the Protestant monarchy that began with William and Mary. The creole class so established at the beginning of the eighteenth century enacted a series of penal laws to deprive the Catholic mass of the

23

population of civil and religious rights and liberties and to exclude them from access to landed property or political power. Many of the remaining Catholic-owned estates were broken up by the laws which discriminated against Catholic inheritance, and a very large part of the Catholic gentry and aristocracy went into exile, to serve the Stuarts and hope for their return, in vain.

The mass of Catholics, four-fifths of the island's population, began to rally in the later eighteenth century, led by rural agitators, priests, a few of the Catholic gentry, members of the new Catholic middle class, and dissident members of the Protestant ruling class, in a variety of movements of protest, rebellion or political agitation. Two dreadful events added bitterness to these agitations, the widespread bloody uprisings of 1798 and their ferocious suppression, and the Great Potato Famine of the 1840s. The power which maintained the colonial regime in Ireland was British. The agitation against that regime took on the colour and the character of nationalism.

In Ulster, the plantation of the opening decades of the seventeenth century, together with later movements of colonization, had settled what became a quite numerous colony of farmers and craftsmen, drawn from Scotland as well as England. The Ulster Presbyterians suffered discrimination and deprivation of civil rights under the penal laws of the eighteenth century, although not as severely as the Catholics. They had much reason for discontent, but, with the redress of their principal grievances by the end of the century, they returned to support of the regime in Ireland, and, ultimately, by the 1830s, to make common cause with the Anglicans, of high and low degree, against Catholic aspirations. Already by the early nineteenth century the Catholic agitation had become democratic in its character, and so – since the Catholics enjoyed a great majority – came to be seen as a threat to all Protestant privilege.

This set the scene for the developments of the past century and a half, developments full of paradox and contradiction. The British system of the eighteenth and nineteenth centuries, embracing Ireland, was oligarchic, anti-democratic, but libertarian. It was also, through the Industrial Revolution and its consequences and related developments, the most effectively modernizing in the world, not politically but socially.

Britain did not, even under the Union of 1800, govern Ireland in Irish interests, but in English interests (chiefly strategic). Ireland, in spite of the Union, was not admitted to normal membership of the United Kingdom but was governed, from 1801 right through to today (in the North) by a series of *ad hoc* separate and special measures. Within the United Kingdom, England functioned, and was seen, not as a partner of Ireland but as an oppressive enemy – in spite of much well intentioned work by many administrators and statesmen. This arose largely because of persistent Irish resistance, sometimes nationalist in character, to the system within Ireland, which was, on the whole, maintained and supported by British governments.

A major, indeed revolutionary, change took place at the end of the nineteenth century, when British governments (both Liberal and Conservative, but in particular, and more effectively, Conservative), simultaneously lost the will to keep repressing resistance and lost patience with the creole landowners, and proceeded, in a controlled and measured way, to distribute the landlords' lands to the tenant farmers. This had the effect of undermining the colonial apparatus of Protestant state control in most of Ireland. A Catholic middle class, which gained legitimacy from its judicious waving of the green flag on appropriate occasions, stood by, ready to take over from the Protestant middle class in the greater part of the island. The takeover process lasted for about half a century. It was strongly and effectively resisted by the Protestant middle class in Ulster aided by the Protestant working class and by the landowning ascendancy. There was neither unanimity nor homogeneity in Protestant Ulster but there was solidarity.

It is important to recollect that in Ireland in general, late to urbanize, a well-rooted bourgeoisie was lacking. The Protestant gentry, arrogant and arbitrary though it often showed itself to be, was yet weak, commanding no prestige among the people and only such force as the imperial government permitted it. There was a patchy but extensive modernizing infrastructure by the end of the nineteenth century, attended by a growing army of functionaries who formed, together with small manufacturers, comprador merchants and an array of middlemen and jobbers, an insecure and uneasy middle class. Within this class, competition for economic survival was not so much entrepreneurial as factional, and very often the factions were denominational. It was the competition of insiders and outsiders, those protected by government and those excluded by government.

Ulster was different. Where most of Ireland had been quicker to anglicize than to modernize, Ulster, east Ulster at least, had modernized and had been transformed in the early stages of the Industrial Revolution. Dublin was the capital, the seat of a government and bureaucracy which, Union or no, retained an essentially colonial character. Belfast was a provincial city, but in its economy it was a British provincial city, integrated into the economy of the Empire rather than into that of Ireland. A maritime city, it was building the greatest ships in the world round the turn of the century and so, both in symbol and in substance, it was a manifestation of the great British thalassocracy. A small, crude, but true bourgeoisie was firmly allied both with the remnants of feudalism and, politically, with the aspiration to a world-wide business-like federation of English-speaking peoples, the vision of many imperialists. By its industry and commerce it dominated its region and in size of population it rivalled, and even briefly surpassed, the decayed and slum-ridden city of Dublin.

In Ulster too, self-reliance was preached in the years before and after 1900: the Protestant ideology taught that the prosperity of Belfast was due to the sterling qualities of a paragon of humankind, the 'Ulster Scot'. The Ulster Scot was in large part a product of the racialist and social-Darwinian thinking of the time. He (very much 'he' rather than 'she') was a Celt, but of a different breed from the soft and volatile Southern Irish. He was steadfast, principled, stubborn, enduring, able to take orders and follow them, a first rate soldier, God-fearing, canny and capable: the stuff of pioneers, explorers, builders of nations. And Protestant self-reliance went back to the very essence of the Reformation. The Protestant read God's word in the Bible and then faced God alone, responsible on his own behalf. God, for the Ulster Protestant, was not mediated by priests, but spoke directly from Mount Sinai. The Ulster Protestants, however, did not aim at political independence. They felt themselves to be partners of the English in the building and management of the Empire, and beneficiaries of imperial trade. This may not seem to be greatly different from the aspirations of Redmondite nationalists before the Great War. But they were convinced, not only that Home Rule would be Rome rule, but also that it would threaten to subordinate them to a backward rural economy and that it could be the first stage of the break-up of the Empire. In short it would raise the inferior above the superior.

To sustain their argument and their confidence it was necessary for them to speak and act frequently as if the population of Ulster consisted wholly of right-thinking 'Ulster Scots'. Of, if they had to, admit the existence of a large number of wrong-thinking people in Ulster; yet, they too had to be assimilated. St. John Ervine, in his biography of Craigavon, attributed to him, accurately enough, no doubt, views he strongly held himself:

> He was two persons: an Ulsterman and an Imperialist. What he did not appear to be, was an Irishman. Ulster was an entity to him. So was the Empire. But Ireland was not. Ireland, in his estimation, was divided into two parts: the North and the rest; and those who were born in Ulster, whether they were Protestants or Roman Catholics, were entirely different from the others. He might even have acknowledged his belief that they were better.

Such a view is not wholly foreign to the thoughts of Ulster Catholics. But Ireland and Ulster are more complex than that.

3

A Short History of Constitutions

The Act of Union, which came into effect on the first day of the nineteenth century was a failure. The Irish nationalist tradition holds that it was bound to fail. But this is not self-evident. One of the more interesting questions to be asked about the modern British nation-state is: why did Ireland turn out so differently from Scotland and Wales? The question is still with us.

We learn from *1066 and All That* that the Irish Question gave so much trouble because the Irish kept changing the question. There is a grain of truth in the witticism. But is might be said with much more truth that the English kept changing the answer.

Down the centuries, Ireland has been given a remarkable number of constitutions, many of them in answer to the Irish Question. In the reign of Henvy VII, Poynings's Law of 1494 subjected the summoning and the legislative programmes of Irish colonial parliaments to the approval of the King of England, then 'Lord of Ireland'. Henry VIII abandoned the Lordship (which originated in Papal grants) and took the title 'King of Ireland', ratifying it through the acknowledgment of the Irish lords and chiefs, to whom he re-granted their lands and gave titles. After the Tudor conquest, Ireland was affected by the vacillations of English politics. During the civil wars the country, or a large part of it, provided itself for a few years with what amounted to a Catholic constitution, before it was subdued again by the English republic – and was brought for the first time, under Cromwell, into a parliamentary union with England.

The distinct Kingdom of Ireland, however, returned with the Restoration. Under George I, 'An Act for the better securing the dependency of Ireland on England' subordinated the Irish parliament to the parliament of the new United Kingdom of Great

Britain. This Act of 1719 was repealed in 1782, when legislative independence was restored. Then, by the Union passed in 1800, the Irish parliament was abolished and that of Great Britain enlarged to receive Irish representatives in a new parliament of 'the United Kingdom of Great Britain and Ireland'. A major amendment of the Act of Union took place with the Act of 1869 which disestablished the Church of Ireland. Then came the succession of Home Rule bills, beginning in 1886.

The third Bill, of 1912, became law in 1914, but was suspended in its operation because the United Kingdom had just joined in the Great War. The Act never came into operation, but was replaced by the Government of Ireland Act 1920, which partitioned the island and purported to set up two subordinate governments, of 'Northern Ireland' and 'Southern Ireland' (six counties and twenty-six counties). Those parts of the Act which related to Southern Ireland were repealed in consequence of the Anglo-Irish Treaty of 1921, as a result of which the Irish Free State came into being in 1922. The Irish Free State enacted its own constitution, but was required to embody in it the articles of the Treaty and also to submit it for British approval. An Anglo-Irish agreement of December 1925 ratified the existing Border between Northern Ireland and the Irish Free State. In 1936, the parliament of the Irish Free State, on the occasion of the abdication crisis in Britain, passed an Act which transferred the prerogatives of the Monarch to the Executive Council of the Irish Free State. In 1937 Éamon de Valera drafted a new constitution which was passed by referendum in the Free State. It gave *de facto* but not *de jure* recognition to the partition of 1920.

This constitution did not require amendment when the Irish Government had an Act passed in 1948 declaring a republic, outside the Commonwealth. A British Act in response (The Ireland Act 1949) recognized that the new 'Republic of Ireland' (its official designation in British law) was a sovereign independent state. The British Act, however, went on to declare that 'notwithstanding that the Republic of Ireland is not part of His Majesty's dominions, the Republic of Ireland is not a foreign country for the purposes of any law in force in any part of the United Kingdom or in any colony, protectorate or United Kingdom trust territory . . .' The Act also declared 'that Northern Ireland remains part of His Majesty's dominions and of the United Kingdom and it is hereby affirmed that in no event will Northern Ireland or any part thereof cease to be part of His Majesty's dominions and of the United Kingdom without the consent of the Parliament of Northern Ireland.'

For fifty years the amended (Home Rule) Government of Ireland Act 1920 served as the constitution of Northern Ireland, but after the suspension of 1972 it was replaced by an Act of 1973, setting up the Assembly which collapsed in 1974. Since then the position of Northern Ireland, under direct rule from a British ministry which replaced the Stormont government, has been uncertain. The relationship between Northern Ireland and Great Britain has been a matter of unfinished business, all sides agreeing that present arrangements are temporary and tentative. The unusual treaty made between the Republic and the United Kingdom in 1985 – the Hillsborough 'Agreement' – has tended if anything to introduce further ambiguity into both the constitutional position of Northern Ireland and the interpretation of the Irish Constitution. It may, however, be a fruitful ambiguity.

The Hillsborough Agreement might be compared with Henry VIII's policy of 'Surrender and Regrant'. Medieval Ireland was, in English eyes, a lordship of the English Crown. The King of England was styled, not King but Lord of Ireland, and was recognized as such by the loyal colonial communities who lived in a number of towns and in the 'English Pale' around Dublin, and who were descended from settlers of the twelfth and thirteenth centuries.

Beyond the limited colonial area, the theory of the Lordship was maintained tenuously and precariously through the mediation of powerful magnates who nominally represented the Lord of Ireland. But they were semi-autonomous, and conducted their complex business with Gaels, Hiberno-Normans and English townspeople through their personal and family relationships.

Henry VIII tentatively began what was to be the long-drawn-out process of extending central government. He ended the reign of the proud vassals who, in his name, managed the country's affairs to suit themselves. The fall of the house of FitzGerald marked the beginning of conquest. When Henry took to himself the title 'King of Ireland' he proceeded to deal with the Gaelic chiefs, whose right to be 'captains of their nations' was immemorial and was backed by genealogies traced all the way to Adam and Eve, by inviting them to surrender that right to him. In return they were granted English titles and were to hold their land from the King. Both they and Henry, by this procedure, flouted Irish law, but there was some short-term advantage for both sides.

For Henry the policy bought time. He had neither the financial nor the military means to venture on a full-scale conquest. He divided the beneficiaries of his grants from their kinsmen, who had no incentive to accept the validity of the grants. The policy bought time but stored up trouble. The subsequent conquests, by diplomacy, plantation and warfare, were to involve great bloodshed in campaigns which verged on genocide.

A curious symmetry marks the final chapters of the long story of the unsuccessful English efforts to rule Ireland. The symmetry shows in the tissue of ambiguities that has characterized the process of English withdrawal over the past century and a quarter. Always, through the best part of five centuries, the English in Ireland have found themselves dealing with collectives difficult to match in any of the estates of their own realm – from the great chiefdoms of O'Neill and O'Donnell to the modern fiefdoms of Hume and Paisley.

Everything English suffers a sea-change on the passage to Ireland, including in particular the law. Even the Union, under which the anglicization of Ireland was completed, did not fully integrate Ireland into the British system. There remained, for example, a Viceroy, a separate executive, a centralized paramilitary police force, housed in barracks and functioning in part like a garrison in occupied territory, and a whole series of separate laws, mostly coercive.

British withdrawal has proceeded in stages, through Catholic Emancipation (the recognition of a large element alien to the Protestant Constitution), the modification of tithe, Disestablishment, the Land Acts, the Home Rule bills, the Government of Ireland Act 1920, the Anglo-Irish Treaty, the Statute of Westminster, the Anglo-Irish Agreement of 1938, the Ireland Act, the suppression of Stormont, the Sunningdale Agreement, and now the Hillsborough Agreement.

The ambiguity of the Anglo-Ulster relationship is shown, on the one hand, in the assertion that Northern Ireland is part of the United Kingdom and in the insistence on Westminster supremacy; on the other hand, in the distancing from Northern Ireland manifest first in long periods during which Northern Ireland was ignored and, more recently, in a variety of special 'colonial' provisions for the province ranging from the use of plastic bullets and CS gas (never so far used in Great Britain) to the curious assumptions of the Prevention of Terrorism Act (for which, for certain purposes, the Irish, North and South, are one and are different from the British).

The Republic's attitude to Northern Ireland has its own ambiguities. Until recently at least, most people in the twenty-six counties would have liked to see an independent united Ireland, but many of them, at the moment, would say: 'Not yet'. This is partly because of the mixture of bewilderment and revulsion that has grown over the past score of years, partly because of the pressure of immediate and serious economic concerns, partly because of propaganda. A certain distancing is in evidence here too, and the Hillsborough Agreement is sufficiently tenuous, imprecise and procrastinating to be acceptable to this tendency. That is, so long as the Northern situation does not deteriorate too badly because of the Agreement. The population of the Republic had a mixed reaction to Hillsborough. Some were firmly opposed to it on the grounds that it appeared to give formal recognition to British jurisdiction in Northern Ireland and so to renege on the aspiration to national unification; a few firmly supported it as a realistic move towards the achievement of peace and rationality in Ireland; a narrow (but soon growing) majority gave it a very cautious 'wait-and-see' appraisal, a provisional approval.

The Agreement itself is about as tenuous as could be. Whatever force it may come to have will depend, not on the enforcement of its provisions, since there is hardly anything in it that is, strictly speaking, enforceable, but rather on the way the two governments choose to use it as a basis for their joint – or separate – approach to the internal problems of Northern Ireland. It is a foot in the door for the Irish government, rather as Henry VIII's Surrender and Regrant policy was a foot in the door. The door could be slammed, by the British government, or possibly by the unionists, with painful consequences. Henry VIII's policy was the beginning of a process that led to warfare of a particularly ferocious character. The Hillsborough Agreement, a stage in the British withdrawal from Ireland, has not ended violence in its first few years; it could undoubtedly, through a little maladroitness, lead to great bloodshed.

It is not the first foot in the door for the Irish government. A toehold was gained with the British admission, after the 1972 suppression of Stormont in favour of proconsular rule, that there was an 'Irish dimension' to the Northern problem. Then Sunningdale brought the Irish government actively into the arrangements for the future of the province. The Sunningdale Agreement collapsed after the Ulster Workers' Council strike of 1974. But the strikers won a pyrrhic victory. Paralysing the province did great damage to the economy of Northern Ireland. For example, it discouraged the foreign investment that was being vigorously and successfully canvassed by John Hume up to the time of the strike, and the discouragement was effective for about a decade. It pointed up the many divisions among unionists, leaving the strikers and paramilitaries in particular deeply resentful of the politicians (including Paisley) who were seen to make capital from the risks and endeavours of other people. And its lesson was not at all clear. Had Protestant Ulster in its righteous might said a resounding 'No!' both to power-sharing *and* to the Council of Ireland? This is very doubtful. A great many middle-class unionists resented being at the mercy and the behest of paramilitaries on the streets.

A widely held view of the strike is that its success was due chiefly to the pusillanimity of Harold Wilson, who hesitated too long without acting and then weakly yielded, not so much to the power of the strikers as to Sir Frank King's reluctance to attempt overcoming their obstruction with the military and police forces at his disposal (which included two very uncertain elements for this purpose, the UDR and the RUC). Further Labour Party dealings with the Ulster question have reinforced the impression of shilly-shallying – notably the deal which James Callaghan, aided by Michael Foot, made with the unionists in order to hang on to office (when they increased Northern Ireland representation in the House of Commons).

33

With the Hillsborough Agreement the Dublin presence in Northern Ireland is quite different from what was envisaged at Sunningdale. There is no doubt that the whole unionist community, of all shades, was strongly opposed to Hillsborough and angry at how the treaty was negotiated over its head. The ensuing mini-election which resulted from the resignation by the Northern Ireland unionist members of their Westminster seats registered this solidarity. That election should be read, not as a normal parliamentary process, but rather as a new covenant binding the Protestants together in opposition to the strangely novel constitutional arrangement which they now faced. As such, it has been a failure.

Before Hillsborough, the Irish government, with others concerned, spent a great deal of time and effort examining, not Anglo-Irish relations as such, but the different question of future internal Irish relations, cast in several kinds of nationalist mould. Although the report of the New Ireland Forum is equipped with detailed and painstaking factual analysis, it is in the end an evasive document. Mrs Thatcher's 'Out, out, out' of 1984 to its several minimal proposals was, as much as anything else, an assessment of the weakness of the whole exercise. The Irish government had wholly renounced the use of force in respect of the Northern problem (an unusual act on the part of a sovereign government in relation to what it regards as a central question of national policy). The British government, meantime, imposes its own current solution of the same problem by force, as witness the armoured cars, military patrols, check-points, helicopters and electronic surveillance in Northern Ireland. It assumes this as the normal prerogative of government. Negotiation between the Irish government and the British on these matters, therefore, proceeds on a basis of great inequality, and the Irish government by its renunciation of force may seem to have increased the inequality. But it is not without moral and other resources, and it is not facing an implacable opponent.

Now, with Hillsborough, two related but distinct long-term problems have come into dangerous conjunction: the question of Irish unity and the question of the British presence and role in Ireland. Dublin has entered, on sufferance, into the government of

Northern Ireland, where, however, the British claim full authority. The nationalist part of the Catholic population does not fully acknowledge British right to govern there, but, for the moment, like the population of the Republic, is divided between those who reject Hillsborough and those who are prepared to give this unusual Anglo-Irish enterprise an extremely cautious provisional approval.

The Protestants opted out, but could not unite on tactics. They have not succeeded in coming to grips effectively with a frustrating and baffling opponent – British government taking Dublin advice on their affairs. It has brought home to them the unpleasant truth that, having lost their measure of local self-government in 1972, they suffer a greatly diminished ability to influence British decisions on matters concerning their province.

They come up against a familiar difficulty in Anglo-Irish relations: Ireland, including loyalist Ulster, is seen by the English as a different place, inhabited by different people, where from time to time paternalistic indulgence has to give way to the firm application of stern common sense – the common sense, of course, and the application being English.

This can lead to cross-purposes, and these too are familiar in the history of Anglo-Irish dealings. Political and constitutional structures are seen very differently when looked at from opposite shores of the Irish Sea. It is arguable, for example, that the British Constitution is a convenient fiction; that close examination will reveal no real fundamental British law that is not subject to arbitrary change – other than the somewhat metaphysical prescription of the supremacy of Parliament. Yet the loyalty of the more fervent and extreme Ulster loyalists is devoted, not to Parliament and its enactments, but to a Protestant Constitution established through the binding together of monarch and people in an implied but real and fundamental covenant.

The covenanting undertone in Ulster loyalist attitudes to the Constitution is important. The Protestant Monarch is both the symbol and the embodiment of the social contract. The Monarch is the personal guarantee of Protestant liberties, and the people, having yielded, for the common good, a part of their freedom to the state, receive back, under that guarantee, their full liberty of conscience, full petitionary access to the Throne, and the capacity to make their own laws subject to – and in partnership with – the Crown. The Monarch, too, has accepted limitations on freedom of action. It is a bargain.

As against this, the majority of the people of Ireland, in the early part of the century, voted, not for a kingdom of Ireland distinct from the United Kingdom of Great Britain; not, in other words, for the constitutional arrangement of the seventeenth and eighteenth centuries; not for Arthur Griffith's 'dual monarchy'; but for a republic, wholly separate from Great Britain. And a Republic is what they achieved.

The distinction is fundamental. Americans today may 'ooh!' and 'ah!' in large crowds at visiting members of the British royal family; they may follow narrations of the real or fictitious lives of royal persons as avidly as they do those of pop stars or baseball players; they may take a keenly snobbish interest in everyday episodes in Buckingham Palace or in the minor misadventures of royal infants; but the fabric of society in the United States of America is republican through and through. There is no New Year's Honours List, there are no earls, dukes, baronets or knights, there is no prescribed formal obsequiousness for public occasions; there is no Established Church; pomp and ceremony are openly and cheerfully spurious rather than groaning under a weight of (equally spurious) sacred history. This is what most of Ireland has chosen. The choice perhaps was unreflective – almost accidental – when it was made, within a period of a few years in the second decade of the century. But it is now established. Once the conjuror's tricks have been revealed, the conjuror loses his mystery and his command.

This is a part of the political problem in Ireland. There is an opposition between republicans and royalists, and the Crown may well be as difficult an item when Northern Ireland's political future is being decided as it was when that of the twenty-six-county State was being bitterly debated many decades ago.

4

Liberty and Democracy

The more committed loyalists share with moderate unionists the
common belief that they live, in the Union, under a system that
secures freedom and democracy better than the system south of the
Border. This view is not shared at all by the nationalists of the
North, many of whom consider that they live under tyrannical
oppression, enforced daily and hourly on their streets by an
occupying army of 'foreign mercenaries' (a term I have heard used
more than once in Belfast in anguish and anger).

That people should understand their own political circumstances
in such strikingly different ways is in itself the kernel of the problem.
It is not surprising that observers from outside Northern Ireland
should lose patience from time to time and incline to Winston
Churchill's view (speaking in the House of Commons in 1922) of:
'. . . the dreary steeples of Fermanagh and Tyrone emerging once
again. The integrity of their quarrel is one of the few institutions
that has been unaltered in the cataclysm which has swept the world.'
But the impatience is not wholly justified. The integrity of the
quarrel is not maintained wholly by stubborness nor is its permanence a fact of nature. It is in the long run a question of politicss.

Politicians and commentators south of the Border like to refer to
Northern Ireland as a failed political entity, a 'political slum' and the
like. Peter Barry when he was Minister for Foreign Affairs in the
FitzGerald government pointed out that democracy had withered in
Northern Ireland. Charles Haughey, as Taoiseach, has more than
once commented on similar failure.

Ever since Northern Ireland came into being as a separate
political unit, with its Home Rule parliament and subsequently
without it, conditions there have been unfavourable to the
development of the Western style of parliamentary democracy
(which is what is being referred to). And the violence, repression

37

and murder of recent years have made such development all but impossible.

That is a special case. It is less obvious, but probably true, that democracy has been withering, more slowly, throughout the Western world. Our crisis is different from that of the 1920s and 1930s. We are not faced with the rise of fascist dictatorships in Europe, or with influential opinion in the parliamentary countries favouring fascism at home. The Second World War ended that phase, and the small neo-fascist movements that now exist enjoy little prospect of success.

We face something different. In the first place, the mechanisms of democracy have changed, and with them, almost certainly, democracy itself. This is a history in which Ireland should have a special interest. The country witnessed some of the most important political experiments leading to modern mass democracy, in the O'Connellite campaigns for Catholic Emancipation and the Repeal of the Union more than a century and a half ago. The Irish democracy was in advance even of the American in that pioneering period. And Irish agitations went on to play a large part in forcing some profound modifications in the English oligarchic tradition of government in the nineteenth century – although that tradition remains strong and English political life has been very slow to develop a truly democratic character. Strauss's work of several decades ago, *Irish Nationalism and British Democracy*, illuminated the relationship. He showed, for example, how significant Irish immigrants were in the Chartist movement.

The poor Irish who flocked to Britain in the middle of the nineteenth century looking for work encountered such difficulties with their longer established fellows – the British natives – as their kind always do. They were, after all, prepared to undercut at the bottom of the labour market. But they also brought with them the healthy spirit of rebellion and dissent and a deep-rooted Catholic suspicion of Protestant cant and hypocrisy. They were a useful leaven in the generally Nonconformist movements towards social justice that were to produce the British labour and socialist groupings of the late nineteenth century. They were outsiders. They were mostly ignorant and illiterate but they had been taught – by their very alienation – some principle of self-help, even if it involved no more than a murderous rejection of all oppressors. They had glimmerings of democracy. Ultimately it was democratic force, backing the physical force of 1916 and 1920, that brought about such independence as was achieved in Ireland.

The Irish State came into being not only with the active participation of a majority of the people within its area (if only through their votes) but with the full expectation of continued participation. It has been one of the strengths of the State until fairly recently that the great majority of its citizens felt that it was theirs (in much the same way that most Americans feel about the USA) and that in one way or another they had quite a say in how it should be shaped. For most, with independence, there ceased to be a sense of alienation from government and from the institutions of public order. This sense of participation is very different from the sense of the English in possession of their Monarch and their government. It is comparatively rare and it is important.

At this point a distinction between democracy and liberty should be noted. They are often confused in casual discourse, because they are related. Although a tradition of liberty is certainly rooted in Ireland, it was never as firmly established there as in England and America. A large repressed majority found a way to assert itself. It demanded, and therefore valued, liberty. But its understanding of liberty appears to have been limited. That is a separate issue from democracy – the participation of the maximum number of people in the public business.

The symbol of such participation has been the vote. In the British political system, which functioned throughout Ireland for a century and a quarter under the Union, the franchise was extended, fairly steadily, through a series of reforms. The first major significant reform came with the Act of Union itself, which did away with the old rotten boroughs (in Ireland but not yet in England) and gave representation to the counties and to the larger cities and towns. But only a comparatively small number of people could vote in parliamentary elections, a number that was temporarily diminished in 1829. Then, stage by stage, that number was increased, as property and other qualifications were abolished. By the 1880s the franchise had widened to most adult males.

By the time of independence, adult females had the vote too (the first woman elected to the Westminster House of Commons was a Sinn Féin abstentionist, from an Irish constituency), and in due course all citizens over 21 years of age (and ultimately over 18) could participate. And by then, in Ireland, the system of pro-portional representation by means of the single transferable vote was giving a fair and accurate representation in parliament of the people's choice.

However, the vote in itself, although an important symbol, is not a great deal more than a symbol. What makes a living democracy is the right, the ability and the incentive to take an active part in the process not only of electing representatives but of directing policy. Assemblies, lobbyings, meetings, torchlight processions, even minor riots; these are the milieu of democracy. Democracy, like any other political system, has its dangers. In the eighteenth century libertarians feared and warned against the rule of the mob as another form of tyrrany. These fears have not been wholly justified in the event, but the question raised is a very pertinent one in Northern Ireland.

The changes of recent years, as they affected democratic systems in the West, are connected, like so many other changes in our lives, with the revolution in communications. Political public meetings and rallies have lost their importance. The selection of political candidates happens differently. This is very noticeable in the American conventions to select presidential and vice-presidential candidates, and it is impossible nowadays to observe at close hand the long-drawn-out presidential electoral processes without feeling that something has gone badly wrong.

Not so very long ago there was usually much uncertainty as to who would be the candidate of each of the two large parties, up until well into the convention. The criticism then made of the procedure was that the election was made through hard bargaining by groups of professional politicians in the notorious 'smoke-filled rooms' away from the public clamour of the convention hall itself.

This was felt to be undemocratic, because private. But now the selection is usually made by other processes, before the convention meets. These other processes are partly electoral, but in a very curious way. The candidate is a product, market-tested through the primaries, not as a president but as a candidate. Marketing skills have come to dominate in politics. The procedure is akin to that by which, in the world of the mass media, people become famous not for being anything in particular but just for being famous. And nowadays the product is sold chiefly not in the public forum but in the private living room. This American development is not remote from Europe. Something similar is happening in Dublin, Luxemburg and Bonn.

And, oddly enough, although the communications systems now available to us appear to bring politicians into close and direct contact with the people, the effect is quite different. What speaks to us from the corner of the living room is no longer a person but a coloured shadow on a glass screen, flattened, boxed, framed, diluted, plasticized, controlled by invisible producers and floor-managers. Alienation returns.

And the image on the screen, like all the other televised images, is a bought one. To communicate with the electorate by the only means nowadays effective is immensely expensive. Fund-raising is the first task of candidacy, and the PACs, in America, are there to provide a large part of the money – 'Political Action Committees', representing special interests (mostly industrial or commercial) who buy future political favours by financing candidacies. Inflated speaking fees for politicians, consultancy fees, and the promise of directorships, chairmanships and so on, all go to the buying as well as the selling of the candidate for office. In America this is combined with a 'private enterprise' system of voter registration that effectively excludes the poor.

There are other reasons for the growing detachment of the ruled from the rulers, even in those countries which appear to continue to practise the 'democratic process'. The notion that might is right, promulgated by the more notorious dictatorships of the 1930s, has returned, in a different form, to the parliamentary democracies of the West today. The doctrine of the survival of the fittest (in its garbled and debased neo-Darwinian form) is dominant again, not in terms of race but in terms of entrepreneurial skill and tough-mindedness. The 'bleeding heart' is eschewed as vigorously by the Reaganites and Thatcherites of today as by the Hitlerites of yesterday. The earth belongs to the strong.

The Irish State came into being largely through a movement of

41

reaction against earlier versions of such ideas. The new State when it was formed, however, was counter-revolutionary and failed to reflect the character of the movement that had brought it into being. The State continued to reflect much of the old order and the old ideas that had been opposed by the movement for independence. Now, as these ideas are coming to dominate in the Republic, larger and larger sections of the population cease to feel the involvement in community that was the essence of Irish democracy and Irish independence.

Paradoxically, although there is much alienation in the North, it is different in character. The violent and impassioned nature of the political confrontation there ensures that – whatever else – people have a sense of involvement in the political world. The 'Troubles' give a meaning to life, if often a very bitter meaning. The people of Northern Ireland are citizens, leading the full human life of participation in those affairs that concern the public good – and disagreeing passionately about where the public good lies. They are prepared for sacrifice and are committed to causes which transcend their private interests. So, although murder is murder everywhere, Belfast is not only a safer place than Washington, DC; it is a more moral place. For the dangers in Washington reflect a society that is meaninglessly self-indulgent in the pursuit of trivial satisfactions; the dangers in Belfast arise from a political culture that recognizes purpose in life.

5

Protestants and Catholics

The undoing of the Union began seriously with the Church Disestablishment Act of 1869. Sixteen years later the first Home Rule Bill was introduced. Ireland's difference was first acknowledged in respect of religion. The move towards political separation followed.

In recent years there have been good studies of Church-State relations, broadly spanning the period since Disestablishment, by such scholars as E. R. Norman, Emmet Larkin, David Miller and John Whyte, among others. The ground is well covered and it begins to be possible to see the wood, not just the trees. It is clear, for example, that the Roman Catholic Church is well integrated into one large section of the Irish democracy, that which has produced the independent State.

Dr Larkin has put forward the interesting view that by the eighties of the last century the coalition constituting the basis of the present Republic had already been formed. It involved the Church as a major element. There is a strong case to be made for this view. However, it must be borne in mind that the term 'Church' here covers a multitude of persons whose views often differed to the point of downright mutual hostility. There is an important distinction to be made, for example, between the ways that lay people have organized themselves to forward the interests of the church or to give expression to 'Catholic ideas' and the ways that bishops have organized themselves for similar purposes.

A main thrust of Catholic endeavour throughout the nineteenth century was the attempt to achieve equality in Irish society, as between Catholics and Protestants. Such equality was not consistent with Protestant privilege. Protestant privilege was sustained by the British connection. This underlies and shapes a great deal of

43

nineteenth-century nationalism. But many Catholics did not want an egalitarian society. What they wanted was that they should not be excluded, on grounds of religion, from privilege, wealth or power. Others did want an egalitarian society and were no happier to contemplate being exploited by a Catholic than by a Protestant landlord or employer. That distinction within the nationalist tradition persists and is quite patent today in the North.

England, where 'Liberty!' was a progressive catch-cry throughout the eighteenth century, was one of the homes of nineteenth-century liberalism. For that liberalism Ireland was a stumbling-block, as America had been in the eighteenth century. To persecute, or even to exclude, people for their beliefs was not consistent with liberal principles. And through the first half of the nineteenth century the strongest Irish Catholic argument was an appeal to those principles. O'Connell, the great Catholic leader, was a Benthamite utilitarian, an active and consistent opponent of slavery, a civil libertarian (which he managed to combine with some prejudices including a vulgar social bias against Jews). Many bishops, too, saw the way forward for their people through the development of British liberal ideas. But that was to assume that Ireland's future lay within the Union, or at least within the British political sphere. Such a future would offer a political advantage to the universal Church, giving a Catholic nation a voice, and a fortuitously powerful one, in the legislature of the major world power of the day.

But there was another scenario. Nineteenth-century liberalism was inherently anti-Catholic (partly because it saw Catholicism in turn as inherently anti-liberal, but partly because of the paradox that liberalism is intolerant of all illiberal philosophies). From the 1860s onward, for a very long time the coexistence of liberalism and Catholicism became extremely difficult. Pope Pius IX's 'Syllabus of Errors' had made virtually all liberal ideas anathema. And the balance shifted in Ireland. Numbers of the Catholic middle class, numbers of the bishops, committed themselves, sometimes cautiously, sometimes rashly, to Home Rule, to devolution, to political separatism. They moved away from the attempt to integrate into British society. They aligned themselves with nationalist discontent.

The Church was seen to be in favour of Redmondite Home Rule. In effect, however, some time after the outbreak of the Great War, the Church withdrew its support from Redmond. He had failed to overcome the Ulster Protestant and unionist opposition to Home Rule, and it looked as if Ulster would successfully break away from the rest of Ireland. For several crucial years the Church was (in effect) politically silent. It was the dog that didn't bark after the Easter rising in 1916.

It barked again in 1922, when civil war followed the founding of the twenty-six-county Irish Free State. The Church now diverged from the lay politicians. Some of the bishops appear to have been more concerned about partition than about the precise details of Ireland's future connection with Great Britain. In the Dáil in that year the priorities were reversed: partition was not the central issue in the debate on the Treaty.

But the bishops were also warily but acutely concerned about the unpredictable forces let loose in a revolutionary situation. They supported the Treaty and the Free State government against the radical republicans (who included in their ranks liberals, communists and dedicated but rebellious Catholics). The government prevailed, at a great cost to public morals and civic benevolence. It established itself through repression, the prospect of a bolshevist or anarchic Republic having terrified the remnants of the old régime into coming to terms with a new ruling class of conservative Catholic lawyers, doctors and shopkeepers.

It was not necessary for the Free State to proclaim a 'Catholic parliament for a Catholic people'. That now existed in fact, and it existed without the nagging worry, such as was to plague Stormont, that the State might be undermined or overthrown by revanchists. Its worries in that respect were brief and concerned the danger of revolutionary levelling. Before Disestablishment there had been a Protestant State for a Catholic people. The thrust now was to turn the tables – not to move towards pluralism. The most consistently pluralist political tradition in Ireland had been the republican, and that tradition remained out of court.

Within a few years of partition, numbers of Protestants had, for a variety of reasons, left the Free State, and the religious balance settled down at 93 per cent Catholic to 7 per cent Protestant. In that situation, the State could afford to be liberal after the fashion of Henry Ford: 'You can have any colour you like so long as it's black.' British parliamentary draughtsmen had written into the successive Home Rule bills a clause prohibiting the endowment by the State of any institution of religion, and this was carried on into the Constitution of the Irish Free State and ultimately into the Constitution of 1937. Its purpose was to prevent a Roman Catholic Establishment, but it was written into the Government of Ireland Act 1920 (which after amendment applied only to Northern Ireland), so that it became the sole clause shared by the constitution of Northern Ireland (which was, until 1972, the amended 1920 Act) and the Constitution of the Republic.

But informally the Church became part of the establishment in two ways. By tacit understanding its voice was effective in two major areas of public policy: education and health. And, in order to have his 1937 Constitution passed – his chief objective being to loosen finally the connection with England – Éamon de Valera, in order not to encounter such opposition as would defeat him on the constitutional referendum, had to seek the approval of the Church and accommodate Catholic social thinking of the time. The time was the 1930s, when much international Catholic political thought was reactionary. There were many in Ireland who aimed at giving full expression in the country to the Catholic 'ethos' of the people. This was strongly argued, for example, by Alfred O'Rahilly, who had draughted a Constitution for the Free State which he published when the enactment of 1937 was being prepared and debated. There were some who admired Mussolini and Franco and, above all, Salazar, and hoped to see a system like theirs established. De Valera was not of their number, but the main opposition party (Cumann na nGaedheal, later Fine Gael) leaned that way.

These people did not draw on the indigenous Catholic tradition, which, after all, had learnt something about the advantages of pluralism within the constraints of the Protestant State. Rather, they were middle-class people who read the fashionable Catholic writers of the day, or the day before, and believed that, since Catholic values were true and good, the imposition of such values would benefit people of all creeds or none. They were not great believers in freedom.

Nor were most of them believers in equality. When straight-

forward professional organizations like the Irish Medical Ass
ation intersected with more equivocal professional-and-busin
associations like the Knights of Columbanus on issues such as tl
Mother-and-Child health scheme of 1951, or, more recently, on
the referendum concerning the insertion into the Constitution of a
prohibition of abortion, they tended to produce a conservative
reinforcement of class divisions.

The Church is not primarily a political institution. But no one has
ever found a wholly satisfactory way to separate religion fully from
politics. The Republic has neither an Established Church, as
England has, nor a formal separation of Church and State, as the
United States has. Somewhere in between, it lives somewhat
uneasily with a semi-established Church and with yet another piece
of unfinished business. It is one of several large areas of Irish
political life where the principles that govern action have not been
thought through.

The overwhelming majority of people of Catholic background in
the Republic has led to assumptions, which are usually but not
invariably unspoken, about the Republic's small religious minority.
Folk-history and myth are involved. Although the Republic is
comparatively free from the kinds of intolerance and prejudice that
bedevil so many societies throughout the world, it is not free from
the self-complacency that begets intolerance. Far too many
expressions of Catholic Irish nationalist have said – in effect: 'Some
of our best friends are Protestants, *but* . . .' The meaning of the 'but'
in this context is that Protestants, however worthy, loyal and
patriotic (after all, many of the outstanding nationalist leaders were
Protestant) still are not quite the real thing, not truly Irish, not
genuinely indigenous, not *echt*-Gaelic.

The important question is whether this vague and usually
unspoken prejudice is founded on a true or a false appreciation of
the nature of the independent Irish State. If it is a true appreciation,
then some very searching questions must be asked about the State
and, in particular, about the State's aspirations in respect of
Northern Ireland. It should be asked, for example, whether
Partition arose not merely from the refusal of Ulster unionists to
come under a Dublin parliament but also from a powerful if largely
unconscious drive by Catholic nationalists to *exclude* Protestants.

There is much evidence – especially since the enactment of partition – to suggest that this might be so.

What actually happens is usually not what people think is happening; what they do is usually not what they say they are doing. *Cui bono?* Partition produced something of a political mess in Northern Ireland. No unionist of any stamp could have been or was wholly happy with the situation that encompassed a major unresolved problem. It was the Southern State that achieved the near perfect definition – over 90 per cent! – of a Catholic nationalist people. And the Republic is dangerously homogeneous. This has increased, not decreased, in almost seventy years of independence. The little Jewish community is diminishing. The number of resident black and Asian people is minute. In all of this, Ireland is strikingly different from most countries of the Western world today.

But it is possible to argue the other way. Compare the Republic with other states that are overwhelmingly Catholic in their cultural tradition or in their actual beliefs and practices – with Poland, for instance (where the proportion of Catholics is almost exactly the same), or with some Latin American countries. If the State had been an overwhelmingly Catholic country formed socially, culturally and politically, in a Catholic mould, it would be quite different from what it is. What it is is an overwhelmingly Catholic state formed, or mainly formed, socially, culturally, and above all politically in a Protestant mould. The very Catholic Church itself in Ireland, in the nineteenth century, took on something of a Protestant character in the effort to achieve a respectable place for its people within an evangelistic Protestant culture. The Irish State is a very curious hybrid, systemically pluralist. This may be changing. The recent upsurge of religious fundamentalism in the world has expressed itself in Ireland in assertions of Catholic triumphalism – most notably through constitutional referendums on abortion and divorce by which, in the 1980s, as counterpoint to the turmoil in the North, Catholic extremists have obtained the pluralities to interfere with the freedom of action of their fellow-citizens. But such victories – which are probably for a short term only – belie the history of the Republic.

That history is such that the importance of the Protestant element in the composition of the State is not to be measured by

48

counting the number of Protestants under the jurisdiction. The small minority of Protestants is essential to the State because they represent its history, and in many respects they represent what gives it meaning.

At the time the State came into being it was customary to interpret questions of nationality largely in terms of race. 'Celt', 'Gael', 'Anglo-Saxon' and other such expressions were current – with reference to the inhabitants of the nation-states of the early twentieth century – and were thought to have meaning in genetic terms. But such notions, although they are still occasionally aired today, have no foundation in reality. There is no one in Ireland today who has any better claim than anyone else to descent from Milesius, Brian Boru, Queen Maeve, Strongbow, or for that matter Oliver Cromwell, whatever the surname, religion or family background. And happily this is not a matter to trouble many people today. But many prejudices are derived from discarded pseudo-scientific notions which live on in the form of unexamined popular ideas. Distinctions between kinds of Irish people, distinctions which attempt to measure degrees of 'Irishness', belong to this category.

If it comes to this kind of dubious competition, there is indeed a case to be made that the loyal Protestant citizens of the Irish State are more truly 'Irish' than the Catholics. In the first place, rather more of an effort is demanded of them to remain citizens, since the environment is slightly out of tune with them. After Partition, many Protestants left the new jurisdiction. Not all left for the same reason, but they must all have felt the drastic change from representing something between a fifth and a quarter of the total population – with close connections for historical reasons with the governing power – to being a very small minority without historical links to the new government. Those who stayed, and their children, had to make a conscious decision to do so in many cases, and a conscious commitment to the State. Often this commitment represented a break with family tradition. They have been well described by one of their number, the late Jack White, in his book *Minority Report*. How they fare is observed by the Protestants of Northern Ireland.

In the second place, the history of Ireland is not the history of a Catholic nation – although it has often been represented as such. It is the history of something much more complex. The complexity includes conflicts, oppositions, contrasts, changes and compromises. The compromises produced the State, and they stem from the Protestant tradition in the main. That tradition can claim to be at least as close to the central tradition of modern Ireland as any other. The Irish State is a secular republic with a very heavy Catholic overburden. The Protestants are the leaven without which that State would lack substance.

Ulster Protestants – much more numerous than those in the other three provinces – are by no means a homogeneous group. Throughout their history they have been divided in almost all the ways in which a society can be divided into classes, groups and opinions. There have been religious divides, between, for example, the once-Established Church and the Presbyterians; within the Anglicans; within the Presbyterians; between both and other churches and sects.

There have been political divides of all kinds, into various shadings and groupings of opinion – republican, Whig, Tory, socialist, and so on. There have been divides of ethnic origin, of social and economic class, of location within the province. But, since quite early in the nineteenth century, Protestant Ulster has been drawn together, and frequently forced together, by a single issue which more and more assumed the character of a threat: the possibility of a Dublin, Catholic, government of all Ireland. Why should this be so much of a threat as to bring about an alliance of the most disparate forces, and to suppress 'normal' European developments such as the emergence of a strong labour movement?

It is because the dominant political tradition in Ulster developed differently from the dominant political tradition in most of Ireland. The traditions were not wholly dissimilar in their origins. But the modern concept of liberty was taken up, in Britain and Ireland in the seventeenth and eighteenth centuries, in different ways by different groups. The 'English Constitution', as established by the 'Glorious Revolution' of 1688, is what underlies the broad basis of Ulster unionism of the past century and more, however varied the structures of political thought that have been erected on that foundation.

Irish nationalism, while accepting enthusiastically the concept of liberty, took a different road. It too has much variety, but we can discern two basic ideas. One is that of the separate Irish nation, a separate kingdom, a separate constitution, ultimately a separate republic. The other is the idea of numbers, pluralities: democracy; participation by the ordinary people in politics at all levels.

An Irish Catholic government in Dublin, a real possibility since the 1830s, was seen by Protestants as a threat to individual liberty – that great value of British nineteenth-century progressive thought. Liberal Ulster Protestants in particular (and there were many) shared in the climate of British political opinion, were interested in British politics, and looked to British developments for the reforms they desired. They became suspicious of Catholic-led or Catholic-manned movements for undoing the Union. And, by the late nineteenth century, industrialized north-eastern Ireland was quite out of step with the impoverished west and with most other parts of the island. Everything that happened after the introduction of the first Home Rule bill in 1886 tended to widen rather than to narrow this fundamental division in Ireland.

And the great variety of political opinion among Ulster Protestants began to be blurred as the aim of preserving the Union obliterated other distinctions. Meanwhile, east Ulster was integrated not only into the British economy but into the British ethos, through common experience in empire-building and war. A very heterogeneous body of people developed a powerful sense of fundamental shared interests, and while they shared some of these interests with the unionists of all-Ireland they did not share them all.

The people of Northern Ireland as a whole live together as neighbours, day by day, and have many common concerns. But there are two distinct communities, intermingled, not joined. Their differences from the rest of the country are in reality much less than they once were. But neither can, in present circumstances, either form a nation or comfortably function as part of a nation, whether British or Irish. The more consolidated community is the Protestant, cut off to a certain extent – by British decisions, British practice and British attitudes – from Great Britain, and therefore all the more dependent on mutual support. And that community faces a real threat. The IRA claims that it is not making war on Protestants. But, following a kind of crazy legalism that has frequently characterized Irish republicanism, it designates as 'legitimate targets' all who wear or have worn the Queen's uniform, or serve the British establishments in Northern Ireland. Since the British have shrewdly 'Vietnamized' the conflict (to borrow a term from a very different situation), Ulster Protestants are in the front line of British Northern Ireland, and they die. The community draws closer, finding cause to cry 'genocide!' The Border is redrawn in blood.

It is really only since the present 'Troubles' began that it has been common in the Republic even to think of the Northern Catholics as a minority. Before that, while it is perhaps true that people rarely thought about them at all, when they did, it was as part of the national majority. The minority group in this view, then widespread, were the Protestant unionists. They were thought of as people misled by propaganda who had allowed themselves to be used when Britain imposed an unnatural partition on Ireland. They were also thought of as people who imposed, on their own part, a bigoted and oppressive regime on the North, in spite of the clearly and democratically expressed wishes of the Irish people.

This in itself shows that there is in Northern Ireland a special case of a situation which is by no means rare, in which majorities and minorities overlap. Those examining the situation are tempted to choose whichever constituency suits their own point of view in deciding who is in a minority, who in a majority. In measuring pluralities we may take as our area of measurement the old United Kingdom of Great Britain and Ireland; or the island of Ireland; or the province of Ulster as a whole, with nine counties; or the six counties of Northern Ireland as delineated in the Government of Ireland Act 1920 (an area defined quite arbitrarily for the purposes of that Act). Or we can attempt a finer analysis and reckon local majorities and minorities by parish or electoral ward.

This is also a case – again of a type not excessively rare – in which *categories* of person overlap: Catholic and Protestant; nationalist and unionist. Not all Catholics are nationalists; not all Protestants are unionists; yet the terms are frequently, if loosely, interchanged. It often suits those whose main interest is religious, as well as those whose main interest is political (on the nationalist side at least), to play down the correlation. This is why vague and pussyfooting terms like 'the minority community' have been added to the large and growing number of euphemisms and evasions by which people have sought to escape some Ulster realities.

One such reality, for almost seventy years past, has been the Border. It defines one area of measurement. North of it Catholics and nationalists are clearly in a minority, nationalists who wish an end to Partition forming, it would seem, about a quarter of the population, Catholics a little under two-fifths. The Border itself, having been in existence for so long now, both marks and creates other realities. There is no overall change in the character of the countryside as one crosses it, but there are lots of changes in detail which were not there seventy years ago. For example, the colours of pillar-boxes, police and military uniforms, and flags change as one goes from south to north or vice versa. These are small but significant matters. And to travel from the Republic to Northern Ireland is to move from a comparatively poor country into the comparatively rich United Kingdom: the quality of the roads, for example, improves strikingly.

The Border was originally drawn to protect and maintain the local Protestant and unionist majority in East Ulster. Since it also includes a large minority of Catholics, there is a question to be asked about them. Is there anything about them which distinguishes them now or has distinguished them in the past from their co-religionists in the other twenty-six counties? The answer must be a very qualified 'Yes'.

Not that the distinction was formerly defined sharply, as it is now by the Border. In the past, the boundary (a cultural divide) was less precise, and enclosed a somewhat larger area, even if it never quite conformed to the boundary of the nine-county Ulster of early modern administrative history. But in many areas in Ulster, and particularly within the six counties now partitioned off, Catholics for several centuries were visibly outnumbered by Protestants. Protestants in turn were too numerous and too well-rooted to appear merely as an imposed group, external to the indigenous community, representing the upper orders of society after a time of conquest and confiscation of property.

In most of Ireland it was possible to envisage the supplanting of the Protestant Ascendancy and the undoing of the conquest through the weight of Catholic numbers. In the North the numbers were not sufficient. The Northern Catholics needed the weight of Catholic numbers in Munster, Leinster and Connacht to accomplish this revolution: it was not one that could be undertaken in Ulster alone. The Northern Catholics, once nationalism had developed to the point where they thought of themselves as the heirs and representatives of the indigenous despoiled and exploited community, could see the Protestants of Ulster as a cuckoo in the nest much bigger than the host bird. To expel the interloper they needed help from outside. And they often viewed it as an expulsion in which there should be no half measures. The great Belfast riots of 1886, for example, on the occasion of the introduction of the first Home Rule Bill, had their obscure origin in an incident on the docks when a Catholic labourer struck a Protestant labourer, telling him that once the Bill was passed, 'none of the Orange sort would get leave to work or earn a loaf of bread in Belfast'.

Elsewhere in Ireland, on the other hand, Catholics working or agitating towards a larger share in the running of the country could feel some confidence in their own superior numbers and could more equably envisage allowing the Protestants a share in power and wealth proportionate to *their* numbers.

The somewhat distinctive outlook of Northern Catholics revealed itself in some shades of difference in their political and organizational behaviour. But it would be a mistake to underestimate the importance of the confessional distinction and antagonism in the history of nationalism throughout Ireland in the nineteenth and twentieth centuries. There is a tendency nowadays, particularly in England, to look on the religious preoccupations of Northern Ireland as an oddity. It is not so long, however, since such preoccupations, and the bigotries accompanying them, were widespread in Britain, in all of Ireland, and most of the rest of the Western world. Asquith, the Liberal British Prime Minister who introduced the third Home Rule Bill and provoked the unionist rebellion of 1912, could refer to the 1908 Eucharistic Congress being arranged for London (as he is quoted in Roy Jenkins's biography) as '. . . this gang of foreign cardinals taking advantage of our hospitality to parade their idolatries through the streets of London: a thing without precedent since the days of Bloody Mary'. In the event the hospitality was not available and the foreign cardinals could not take advantage of it.

In parts of the North, the old Irish parliamentary party which had worked for Home Rule survived the Sinn Féin landslide of the 1918 election much better than it did elsewhere – an indication of a different pattern of political behaviour. The parliamentary party rump, under the leadership of Joe Devlin, gave a peculiar character to Northern politics.

This is not to say that the Ulster Catholics did not sympathize with the struggle for independence in the form of a Republic that was being waged with the assent, if not precisely under the leadership, of Sinn Féin in 1919–21. They did; but as a minority community in Belfast and some other areas they needed the parliamentary party's local political skills much as the Irish immigrants in New York needed Tammany Hall at one time.*

Elsewhere in the country the old Westminster party politics could be abandoned completely. A distinctive dualism developed in the North, which was to characterize the whole island to some degree in the 1920s and 1930s but which was most marked in Northern Ireland. On the one hand, people relied on the parliamentarians for working the system and gaining what advantage was to be gained from the existing political arrangements – although these in principle were not approved. On the other hand, armed republicans were also given sanction as agents of the long-term solution of reunification. They were also recognized as the militia to defend Catholic areas, especially in Belfast, in times of confessional conflict.

The North, especially in the Border areas, remained for a long time a stronghold of the Ancient Order of Hibernians, a watered-down Catholic version of the Protestant Orange Order. The Orange Order itself, once nation-wide, survived in Ulster throughout the fifty years of Northern Ireland's limited self-government. The Orange Institution owed its survival in Northern Ireland probably not so much to the fact that it was a Protestant

---

*Democratic Party organization in New York which became associated with corruption.

organization directed against Catholics – a reputation it has always had amongst the Catholics of Ulster – as, perhaps, to the fact that it provided a means by which lower-class Protestants, deprived by the extraordinary political circumstances of Northern Ireland of the possibility of forming a regular working-class party alignment, could register their views and express them to their betters within the egalitarian convention of the Lodge. The political importance of the Orange Order has diminished dramatically with the opening up of Ulster Protestant politics since 1969.

The politics of Fine Gael and Fianna Fáil – civil war politics – could never truly take root in Northern Ireland. The circumstances there were quite different. The IRA retained among Northern Catholics a respectability which it gradually lost in the South, where it was in competition with the regularly appointed army of the State whose legitimacy was acknowledged by all but a tiny minority of the citizens. For the Northern Catholics, or rather for a large majority of them, on the other hand, the political system to which they belonged was illegitimate; the British Army was not their army; the RUC and the B-Specials were certainly not their police force. In this they were fully encouraged by the public policies and pronouncements, although rarely if ever by the actions, of the Southern State, whether Free State or Republic.

There were, in other words, from long before the foundation of the new State of Ireland, some differences in situation, in outlook and in aspiration between the Catholics of the six counties and the Catholics of the other twenty-six. These differences were increased by partition. For one thing, the process or operation of Partition itself was traumatic for the North, much more so than for the much larger twenty-six-county South. Partition was hardly an issue in the agonized Treaty debate in Dáil Éireann in late 1921 and early 1922. That debate was on fundamental questions of forms of government and allegiance. Partition was left aside largely perhaps because of the hope that the question would be happily resolved by the deliberations of the Boundary Commission, but partly also because it was not of immediate or primary concern to the Deputies who were discussing how to reconcile their oath to the Republic with a new oath of allegiance to the King of England.

Partition, however, was not accepted by the sentiment of

nationalist Ireland of any shade of politics, and the new self-governing province in the North came into being under threat of takeover, under boycott and disapprobation and without acknowledgment or recognition from most of its Catholic inhabitants.

The new Border left sensations of betrayal, or at least of let-down, on both sides of the political and religious divide in Ulster. Many unionists in Donegal, Cavan and Monaghan were bitter because their fellows in the other six Ulster counties had abandoned them for the sake of the smaller but more tenable area to be excluded from Dublin rule. Many Catholic nationalists in those six counties felt that they had been abandoned in the settlement made between Dublin and London. However, they at least, unlike the three-county unionists, could console themselves with the hope that their exclusion would be brief. Partition was seen to be an interim measure. And they could look to a native Irish government in Dublin to bring about the reunification that would restore them to a majority position (they did not at first look to the native Irish government in Stormont for anything, although native Irish it was).

The correlation of religion and politics was very clear at this period, in the first few years of the new sub-territory of Northern Ireland. The Catholics, not just as nationalists but as Catholics, refused to cooperate in setting up the institutions of the new province. Spokesmen of the institutional Church supported this non-cooperation and joined in it themselves, when, for example, the reorganization of the education system was attempted by the first minister, Lord Londonderry.

The Protestant levies of the Special Constabulary were inheritors of the role of the Ulster Volunteer Force of 1913, although they were now established by the British government, not in arms against it. They treated Catholics, *per se*, as enemies of the State. The first three years of Northern Ireland were years of blood, degenerating like the present troubles from paramilitary activity into savage inter-confessional killings. These were mostly directed against Catholics, but they culminated in the assassination of two Unionist parliamentarians. There was for a while the possibility of invasion from the South, but the civil war put an end to that. The Northern Catholics, still seeing themselves as part of the national majority, settled down to wait, first for the Boundary Commission's

57

report; then, when that gave them no comfort, for the favourable development of Southern politics. It was to be a long wait.

6

The Border

Ulster is different. While it is not difficult to trace broad distinctions, in economy, custom and outlook, between Munster, Leinster and Connacht, the distinction is much sharper when it comes to Ulster. This was so before Partition; indeed, to some extent, it was true before the Plantation.

The difference before the Plantation partly showed itself in the archaizing character of the northern province. Since about the tenth century, while the south and east opened up more and more to influences from the larger world, most of Ulster turned in on itself, failed to develop towns and reverted to the cattle economy of earlier times. The Viking presence along the east coast was not maintained, even as far south as the Boyne, and later the Anglo-Normans made a permanent and solid impact only in parts of the coastal areas.

But the Plantation and other seventeenth-century settlement wholly changed this character, although most of the Scots, in particular, brought with them a material way of life not startlingly different from that of Ulster. This, in fact, probably contributed to the comparative success of the settlement. However, new towns were laid out, and new crafts and farming ways were introduced, chiefly by the English planters.

One of the most striking features of the Plantation arose not from its success but from its failure. It had been intended, over large areas, to replace the native population with a new Protestant population. In practice, while Protestants were settled, the native Catholics were only partly displaced, so that a human landscape was formed which was a mosaic of creeds and traditions and a problem was created which is still important in the society and politics of Northern Ireland.

A most significant contrast with the rest of Ireland came from the development later, of the 'Ulster Custom', a landholding system that gave some security to tenants and did not involve the penalties on tenants' improvements which were a vicious and destructive feature of landlordism here and there throughout most of the island. By the later eighteenth century Ulster was already remarked on for the better, tidier, cared-for appearance of its farms, orchards and towns. To an extent, it has maintained this distinction ever since. And with the building of the textile, shipyard and engineering industries in the eighteenth and nineteenth centuries, north-eastern Ireland, by the years around 1900, had come to be strikingly different from the rest of the island.

The contrast is much smaller now, since the smokestack industries that distinguished Ulster before the Great War have long since declined, to be replaced by others, while the twenty-six-county State, especially since the Second World War, in turn developed and changed. A few years ago the Republic had achieved parity with Northern Ireland in productivity and was approaching parity in material living standards. What has happened since then is too much affected by the 'Troubles' to make a continued comparison useful.

It has often been remarked that Ulster reproduces on a smaller scale the morphological features of the whole island. It has an upland perimeter and a lowland interior. The inward drainage produces a feature analogous to the Shannon with its tributaries and its spreading lakes: the Bann, widening out into the great expanse of Lough Neagh and receiving the waters of a number of smaller streams. And like the Shannon, the Bann marks a significant division. However sharp the contrast between North and South in Ireland, the contrast between east and west is in many ways more important.

All this gives Ulster, in relation to the island as a whole, not only a distinctiveness but a tendency to self-sufficiency. The hills, rivers, lakes and bogs that fringe the southern borderlands of Ulster close off the province from the midlands – especially perhaps the hundreds of drumlins, with the little closed-in valleys between them, that swarm from Strangford Lough across to Sligo Bay. The frontier zone also has its own distinctive character and forms one of a number of sub-regions, each with a particular physical, social and political complexion, that add to the complexity of Ulster.

This sub-region is of course the one that is distinguished, as it has been for most of this century, by one of the chief political landmarks of twentieth-century Ireland: the Border. The boundary, which now separates Northern Ireland from the Republic, was first established by the Government of Ireland Act 1920, and came into effect in British law in 1921, when that Act was implemented. The Act, which replaced the Government of Ireland Act 1914 (the third Home Rule Bill as passed into law), partitioned Ireland unevenly, separating 6,000 square miles from 27,000 square miles, and dividing off one and a half million people (of whom at that time about 66 per cent were Protestants and about 34 per cent Catholics) from three million (of whom about 10 per cent were Protestants and about 90 per cent Catholics).

Many people at the time thought that the partition was a temporary expedient. Yet the distinctiveness of Ulster – especially the powerful opposition to Home Rule of the great majority of Ulster Protestants – was widely recognized. Some form of partition had long been mooted. It had been suggested by unionists in Belfast in 1843, at the time of O'Connell's campaign for Repeal of the Union. When Gladstone was introducing the first Home Rule Bill in 1886, he discussed in some detail the powerful unionist objections to his bill and indicated that the measure as introduced was subject to substantial amendment after debate in Parliament – including, if absolutely necessary, the enactment of some form of Partition. But he hoped to avoid that, and pointed out that the Bill proposed a continuation of the Union. An Irish executive would be responsible to a subordinate Irish parliament in Dublin in certain specified and limited Irish internal matters, but Westminster would continue to have ultimate authority and would continue to be directly responsible for matters relating to the Crown, for war and foreign affairs, and for all principal fiscal questions.

That Bill never came to the stage of amendment, since Gladstone's own party, the Liberal Party, split on it and it failed in the Commons. By the time he came to introduce the second Home Rule Bill in 1893 (it was defeated in the Lords), a certain *de facto* Partition had already taken place, not in law but in political reality.

The unionists of Ireland had now organized themselves quite effectively to resist Home Rule, but had also realistically accepted a division in their own ranks. In the nine counties of Ulster, where they could command a local majority, they had a separate organization. The unionists of the other three provinces fought on different ground. There was a fallback plan: at worst, the Union would be saved in Ulster.

By the time the third Home Rule Bill was introduced, by Asquith's Liberal government, in 1912, the power of the Lords to block a Bill had been reduced to a two-year delay. The Liberals, with the Irish party, had the votes to carry the measure in the House of Commons. Now the Ulster unionist strategy was put into effect. The Conservative and Unionist Party sponsored a provincial resistance to the Bill and organized the great display of opposition on 'Ulster Day', 28 September 1912, which concluded when nearly half a million people signed the 'Ulster Covenant'.

They pledged themselves 'to stand by one another in defending for ourselves and our children our cherished position of equal citizenship in the United Kingdom, and in using all means which may be found necessary to defeat the present conspiracy to set up a Home Rule Parliament in Ireland. And in the event of such a Parliament being forced upon us we further solemnly and mutually pledge ourselves to refuse to recognize its authority . . .'

In Munster, Leinster and Connacht there was also unionist opposition to the Bill, but it hadn't the weight to prevail against both the decision of Westminster and the overwhelming nationalist opinion in those provinces. The Ulster Unionist Council, representing the whole of the majority (unionist) opinion of the northern province, was taking what was becoming a quite separate course.

In 1908 a legislative and legal partition had already taken place, making a separate provision for Ulster, when Parliament, in reorganizing the Irish universities system, had joined the Queen's College of Galway and Cork to what was to be University College, Dublin, in a new National University of Ireland (leaving the University of Dublin – Trinity – independent) but had created from the other Queen's College a 'Queen's University of Belfast' which was separate and distinct from the National University. Ulster's difference was given formal recognition.

Now, in the constitutional crisis that followed the third Home Rule Bill, Ulster's difference seemed likely to lead to civil war in the United Kingdom. The Ulster unionists, threatening to seize independent control of their province should the Bill pass, formed and armed their own paramilitary levy, the Ulster Volunteer Force, and, in due course, in effect faced down the government. This in turn led to the formation of a nationalist armed force. It gave an opportunity to republican revolutionaries whose objectives went far beyond Home Rule. But the unionist combination of a show of force with intrigue and negotiation behind the scenes in London, undid in part what had been achieved by nationalists in Parliament. A temporary partition became the ground of compromise, and the question at issue was: where should the boundary be drawn?

It was the reluctant decision of the Ulster Unionist Council that provided the formula for the Partition enacted at the behest of the British government in 1920. It was done to ensure a two-to-one majority by abandoning the Ulster unionists of Donegal, Monaghan and Cavan. In Ulster as a whole, the unionist majority was too slim to be secure. In other words, Northern Ireland was defined on the basis of an old-fashioned gerrymander. This, of course, apart from the mere fact of the Partition itself, was to create a persistent grievance. The Partition was arbitrary, to suit best the intentions of the unionists of the day. Not that they wanted Partition at all; they wanted to preserve the Union. But if all Ireland couldn't be held in the Union, then they wanted to preserve the Union where they could.

Had the line of division been drawn by some celestial court of arbitration in which simple fairness prevailed, it might have been expected that either nine counties (the province on which the Ulster unionists had staked their claim) or about three would be separated from the rest of Ireland. But the Partition was not arranged by a court of celestial fairness, or by a debating society. These matters never are. Ireland's political shape for half a century was to be decided by the exercise of power – by the unionists, by the nationalists, by the republicans, by the British government. Each employed the ballot-box, the gun and the press to gain political ends.

A new balance emerged and for a while, as we can see in

retrospect, it was a fairly stable balance. No one in Ireland really believed the stability, because no one believed that the balance was final. The Government of Ireland Act 1920 in its unamended form provided for a Council of Ireland 'with a view to the eventual establishment of a Parliament for the whole of Ireland, and to bringing about harmonious action between the parliaments and governments of Southern Ireland and Northern Ireland . . .' The two parliaments proposed under the Act were given powers to establish a parliament of Ireland. The Anglo-Irish Treaty of 1921 recognized for the whole island an Irish Free State, with dominion status – much greater autonomy, in other words – but gave the already existing parliament of Northern Ireland the right to opt out by presenting an address to the Crown.

This was promptly done, and under the terms of the Treaty a Boundary Commission was then to be established to see what revision should be made of the arbitrarily imposed Border (which simply followed old county boundaries). The government of Northern Ireland refused to cooperate on the Boundary Commission, and so caused some delay. In the end, the Border was left unchanged.

Once the new Irish Free State, of twenty-six counties, began to function, the British government was happy to turn its attention elsewhere. South of the Border, while state-building proceeded quite successfully (after the end of the civil war), both popular sentiment and government long-term policy remained irredentist in respect of the North. North of the Border the Unionist government soon found that the extent of territory it had chosen was in fact too large for peace of mind. The nationalists were just too numerous and too hostile to the new arrangement. It was not felt safe to try to draw them into common citizenship with the unionists. The nationalists themselves set their hopes on the South.

The balance then achieved, precariously and, it seemed, tentatively and temporarily, served to make possible a kind of stability for some decades. But that balance no longer exists. The Home Rule arrangement in Northern Ireland collapsed in 1968–1972. The British government promptly intervened with armed force to re-stabilize the province and to re-impose government control. This can hardly be sufficiently emphasized, because the propaganda exercise which represented the soldiers as 'peace-keepers' has been remarkably successful. Of course, in a sense, they were attempting peace-keeping, but it was the Queen's Peace they wished to maintain – government control of an uprising.

They were summoned to the streets, not to act as neutrals between Protestant and Catholic rioters (the conflict at the time was between a popular uprising in Catholic areas and the forces at the disposal of the Stormont government), but 'to the aid of the civil power'. As it happens they were illegally summoned, since the civil power in question was Stormont, the government of Northern Ireland, which, under the Government of Ireland Act 1920, was precluded from their aid. When at a later date the British Army sprayed with dye John Hume, who was taking part in a sit-down civil rights protest, he took to the courts and won his case: the army's actions on the streets had been illegal since its first deployment in August 1969. An interesting piece of retrospective legislation was rushed through Westminster to indemnify the soldiers and save the government from the punitive costs of what could have been a flood of litigation.

This was necessary because a slip had been made in the haste of improvization in August 1969. The soldiers in fact were and are an instrument – the chief instrument – of British policy in Northern Ireland. That policy, after all (like any government policy in the last resort) is imposed by force. It is a policy only parts of which receive the consent even of the unionists; but all of it is imposed by force. The unionists and the loyalists are indeed glad of British power for the maintenance of partition and of the Border; but they don't like the internal arrangements which the same power imposes; they don't like being governed as a proconsular province; above all they don't like having Dublin intervention forced on them with the backing of British power under the terms of the Hillsborough Agreement. They are not given a choice: they must take the one with the other.

The deployment of the British Army on the streets and roads of Northern Ireland was promptly followed by a split in the IRA (into 'Officials' and 'Provisionals') and by a renewal of IRA activity on a scale not before seen in the North. Northern Ireland, after 1969, indeed became a different place, an extremely violent place, different now not only from Great Britain but from the Republic. The Border took on a new character.

It is a border easy to cross, and perhaps that tells us something about it. It does admittedly look intimidating nowadays, especially on the Northern side. The littered foundations of burnt-out customs stations speak of violence. Coils of barbed wire, concrete look-out posts and spindly watch-towers on the hills, sandbags, guns, sinister-looking surveillance lenses; all give a visual impression which is not too far from that made by the Iron Curtain. But train passengers (when the trains are running and not halted by bomb-threats or bombs) do not see this at all. Bus passengers need hardly notice it, and neither they nor people travelling by car are, as a rule, detained or disturbed for more than a moment.

The soldiers in their armoured cars on both sides of the frontier, the unarmed Gardai and the armed RUC, are not confronting one another in a hostile stand-off across the little bridges and meandering streams that are on the ground what is represented by that wriggling line across the map of Ireland. They are collaborating, although across a formal space, and they courteously facilitate the easy passage of the great majority of travellers across the Border. They are not needed there to maintain the Border itself – smuggling, for example, is not generally their concern. They are jointly protecting a common realm against a common threat.

This is a paradox that will bear thinking about. Not thinking about it leads to some confusion, north and south of the Border. It leads some loyalists in the North to look on the chief function of the British Army and the RUC, behind their sandbags and barbed wire, as being that of defending Northern Ireland against raids by Provisionals from their bases in the Republic, or against the columns of Southern armoured cars that might (without such defence) drive through Lisnaskea and Beleek, Aughnacloy and Newry, to dash for the taking of the Belfast city hall and the flying of the tricolour from the topmost spars of the giant gantry, 'Goliath', that towers over the shipyard. It leads some nationalists in the South to the complaint that Ireland's army is being employed to prop up Britain's Border; or, more to the point perhaps, to complain that Gardai who should be apprehending drug-pushers and muggers are wasting their time and Irish taxpayers' money looking after someone else's (Britain's) interests.

All border zones, everywhere, are potential areas of benefit to bandits, smugglers, guerrillas, 'special forces', and other practitioners of black arts and black economies. The Irish Border zone, for a century and a half before it was given formal recognition through the partition, was already an area (not unlike the more formal Scottish Border of the Late Middle Ages) of outlawry and semi-legal activity. It is the zone where the overwhelming Catholic majority of most of Ireland shades into substantial Protestant numbers. It is the zone where, after partition, illegal economies flourished all the better for their situation in a minefield of religious and political bigotries.

What is the common realm defended along the Border by British and Irish forces against what common threat? The threat is not simply that of violence, or armed force as such. Neither the government of the Republic nor that of the United Kingdom is pacifist, and the soldiers on both sides of the Border are quite prepared, in appropriate circumstances, to use the guns they carry. The threat is that of a particular violence, chiefly that of the IRA. The IRA operates primarily from a base of disaffection in the North; but it makes full use of the ambiguities and discontinuities of the Border zone for one part of its activities. Indifferently it raids the North from the South and occasionally the South from the North (although its targets may be different on the different sides of the Border).

The common realm being defended is not so clearly defined. It is the way of life of the kind of people who read the *Irish Times*, the *Guardian*, the *Independent*, *Le Monde*, the *Frankfurter Allgemeine Zeitung*, the *New York Times* and the *Washington Post*. It is the realm of parliamentary democracy, audio systems, wine, experiment, concern about the environment, art exhibitions, books and the second family car. Much has changed since 1920. This realm is worth defending. It is civilized, and for those within it it provides, among other things, what the churches used to provide: guidelines for decent behaviour. But it is a realm much narrower than it looks to many of its inhabitants. It exists within a hungry and deprived world.

'Alienation' sums up the Border. This good Marxist word has most interestingly come in the past few years to the lips of Irish cardinals, bishops, Fianna Fáil entrepreneurs and even leaders of the Fine Gael party. It has become current in Ireland – because it was needed. Alienation, in this sense, can undoubtedly be recognized instantly in parts of West Belfast, in parts of Derry, in Armagh, in Dublin, Cork, Limerick and – among numerous other places – north Kerry. It was clearly manifest in the middle 1980s in the young boys in parts of Dublin who went 'joy-riding' – stealing cars which they drove at high speed and with which they rammed police cars, often enough killing themselves and others. A very similar activity had developed a few years earlier in Ballymurphy and Andersontown in West Belfast. The boys there didn't ram police cars; they drove at high speed through military check-points, causing, through their provocation of the British Army, not only immediate peril to themselves but also considerable bother to and retaliation from the IRA. It was Russian roulette.

'Alienation' means that people feel they are not regarded as whole persons. In their work (if any) and in their society they are treated as 'hands' or as rejects. They are waste-products of the good society, and in Ireland there are many of them. The guns of one state are not directed against the armed forces of the other along the Border. They are all directed against the alienated. Dublin may bargain hard with London about the implementation of the Hillsborough Agreement or other elements of the Northern Ireland problem; but this is like the hard bargaining that goes on in Brussels. It is about the division of the spoils we all take from a hungry world.

The Border zone is also an area of high stress in many other respects. Much of the land among the drumlins is poor, and rural life is hard. The seventeenth-century Plantation left a settlement pattern in which, by and large, Protestants had the better land (mostly in the valleys) and Catholics the poorer (mostly in the hills). Land-hunger, envy, bitter memories of real or imagined confiscations, evictions and expropriations long ago, begrudging and religious bigotry characterize parts of the area. A local man, driving along by the rushy streams between the endless shut-in hogback hills, will know and note every Protestant farm, every Catholic farm, along miles of road.

It was here that serious interdenominational strife began, two hundred years ago, in the fields of County Armagh, when there was a population explosion in the area and consequent desperate competition for subsistence, among farmers who were also weavers. Sectarian secret societies were formed. There was much bloodshed and there were many atrocities. The Orange Order was founded among the Armagh fields after an affray in 1795. Large numbers of Catholics were driven from their cottages to flee from Ulster, to north Longford, or farther afield into Connacht. All this is remembered. In the Border zone there flourished the Catholic Defenders, the Protestant Peep-o'-Day Boys, the Ribbonmen, the Ancient Order of Hibernians, and the stubborn bitterness of Orangeism. It is an unyielding, unforgiving country.

Taking the Border zone as a whole, we are faced with a problem largely derived from the Plantation. Catholics form a narrow overall majority, in a crazy pattern of settlement by which Green and Orange are inextricably interlocked. They are interlocked too in a silent, straining struggle, each striving to dislodge the other. This is largely a struggle over land, as it has been for two hundred years or more.

In the Border areas there have been numerous killings of former or part-time UDR men, often as they left home for work or returned from work. In the same area too, in earlier decades of this century, the armed Special Constabulary – the Protestant 'B-Specials' – earned an evil reputation in their (largely successful) endeavour to keep 'Fenian' rebellion under control. In a countryside where everyone knows a good deal about the movements, and the business, of everyone else, the long history of neighbours murdering neighbours is that of an ancient communal vendetta. Yet they live with one another; even cooperate with one another in many matters. But there is an abiding mistrust and there is an underlying implacable hostility.

Catholics see Protestants enjoying possession of good land that was stolen centuries ago from Catholics. They look to the day when that possession will be vacated. Protestants, righteous in their husbandry of that which came down to them from ancestors who colonized a wilderness, make the Ulster affirmation: 'What we have we hold'. They see their Catholic neighbours as weakminded people too easily provoked by foolish nationalist agitations to murderous treachery. They hold bitterly against even their 'good' Catholic neighbours the *omertà** that through decades and centuries of land wars, rural secret societies and circumventions of law, has protected the cattle-hougher, the barn-burner, the noonday assassin.

The Border has been a war-zone of a kind for the past twenty years. An attempt by the IRA to mount a campaign along it in the 1950s was a failure because of lack of popular support, although at that time people turned out in considerable numbers to vote for, and to elect, Sinn Féin candidates who had been convicted for participation in that campaign. But in the 1950s the IRA were unable to persuade people that their bombings of customs posts, occasional arms raids on British military bases, random pot-shots at the RUC, were anything but futile; especially since they inflicted more casualties on themselves through accident and ineptitude than on their designated enemy.

But the events of the late 1960s and early 1970s changed that opinion. Suddenly it seemed as if there were a real chance of ousting the British from Ireland. Only the British? The IRA proclaimed that it was fighting for all Irish people against a foreign enemy, for a united Irish Republic. It was not campaigning against Protestants as such. But along the Border, in Fermanagh, Tyrone and Armagh, the renewed and greatly enlarged Provisional IRA of the 1970s and 1980s drew its recruits from the local farm and small-town boys, very many of whom had a family tradition not of republicanism but of Hibernianism.† There was some basis for the gibe that the new 'Provies' were 'Hibs with guns'. And the local Protestants, observing the selection of targets, including many heirs to Protestant farms, saw an IRA campaign, not so much against the British Establishment as against the local Protestant tenure of the land. The complaint that genocide was being attempted is not wholly without reason.

But is not as simple as that. For the Border zone includes within

Omertà: Sicilian term for communal silence about illegal actions.
†Hibernianism: associated with the Ancient Order of Hibernians (see p. 55 above).

Northern Ireland large tracts of country and several towns which are overwhelmingly nationalist in their population, and within the Republic districts and towns where the people have a strong sympathy – not shared in the same way elsewhere in the country – with the nationalists of Northern Ireland. So, for example, some of the people in Iniskeen in County Monaghan – an Ulster county – are virtually of one political mind with the people of Crossmaglen, five miles away across the Border in County Armagh. And Crossmaglen is a village under military occupation, a nationalist village in a nationalist countryside, where the British supply their troops and patrol the roads and the Border by helicopter, where they and most of the local population exist in a state of armed enmity, where to an extent there is a re-enactment of the sort of guerilla war that took place in west Cork in 1920 and 1921.* But only to an extent. It is difficult to envisage in Cork in 1920, even as a possibility, anything like the machine-gunning some years ago of the fundamentalist Christian congregation in their tiny chapel in the little hamlet of Darkley in south Armagh (apparently an INLA rather than an IRA atrocity).

At the two extremities of the Border zone of Northern Ireland circumstances are somewhat different. South Down is not quite as homogeneous as neighbouring south Armagh, being more varied not only in Protestant-Catholic terms (although it is mainly Catholic) but also socially and economically. It fits in a way into the near-conurbation of the east coast of Ireland which extends, with some interruptions, from Larne to Bray. The mountain mass of the Mournes is one of the interruptions, but both the main (inland) road from Belfast to Dublin and the coast road run through a string of towns, and Newry, the centre of south Down (a nationalist town) is in an odd way the twin of Dundalk – the eleven or twelve miles between them running through the 'gap of the North', a pass of ancient strategic significance through the mountains.

Newry and Dundalk have that uneasy zero-sum relationship that we find among other twinned towns along the Border. One booms and the other slumps, depending on which way the fiscal policies of the two governments affect the price of petrol, drink and other

---

*West Cork was an IRA stronghold during the War of Independence, 1919–21.

commodities on either side of the frontier. But they have other relationships too. Newry, like almost all towns in Northern Ireland, has had its whole centre blown to pieces by bombs, but has been mostly rebuilt and renewed. Dundalk, across the Border, has served as an occasional refuge for the bombers but, more significantly, as a rest and recreation place for the stressed citizens of Newry from time to time.

Newry had the interesting distinction, even before the 'Troubles', of having a branch of the Irish Labour Party. The political parties of the Republic – with the exception of Sinn Féin, which was generally unable to win any seats in the Republic –hadn't for many years organized in Northern Ireland. The Northern Ireland Labour Party, akin but not affiliated to the Labour Party in Great Britain, was, as it were, passively unionist. That is to say, it tried to remain neutral on the central issue in Northern Ireland politics in the pathetic hope that it could span the religious divide and introduce real class politics into the province (British Labour being consistently blind to the class significance of its own imperialism). It committed suicide in Northern Ireland. The Irish Labour Party, which had an anti-partitionist spasm in the 1960s, had once had a good base in County Louth and had expanded locally from Dundalk to Newry. The party allowed its whole organization in Louth to atrophy, but when it revived in 1965, Newry was again for a very brief period within its sphere of activity. But, in Northern Ireland, more interesting politics soon supervened.

There is a very special case at the other end of the Border: Derry, or Londonderry. It is universally known colloquially as 'Derry', but in formal language 'Derry' is its nationalist name, 'Londonderry' its unionist name: officially the city is now 'Derry', the county 'Londonderry'. The city, the second in Northern Ireland, has a population which is two-thirds Catholic and nationalist. Like Belfast, it was the scene of recurrent serious riots – between nationalists and unionists – throughout the second half of the nineteenth century; but with a significant difference.

Derry had a special mythical and emotional significance for Protestants and loyalists – which Belfast hadn't – because of the special part it had played in the logomachy of the Ulster Protestant memory. It was (to borrow Waterford's town motto) *'urbs intacta'*.

THE BORDER

Ulster Protestants are a people under siege – at least so they have long seen themselves – and Derry was the city of the siege (of 1689). Its walls remain intact, as they were built in the seventeenth century. They withstood the siege of 1689 (initially directed by James II in person), which ensued when the ordinary people of the city closed the gates as their betters, notably the governor, Lundy, were about to make terms with the king, who represented papism and absolutism. The siege of Derry came to symbolize the sense of being beleagered felt by Ulster Protestants in general in the later nineteenth century, and when loyalists sang in the refrain of one of their ballads, 'We'll guard old Derry's walls', they were making a present affirmation about their feeling for Ulster as a whole.

The city was built on the site of an old monastery on a steep-sided hill, almost an island, on the western side of the Foyle. Its immediate hinterland is the mountainous Inishowen peninsula in County Donegal, now in the Republic. After the Plantation the rural population on both sides of the river was largely Protestant and included in parts of eastern Donegal significant numbers derived from settlements of Scottish Calvinists. East of the broad Foyle the County of Coleraine, or Londonderry, had been a special part of the Plantation granted, like the city, to the 'Irish Society' of the City of London. A Protestant urban settlement was to develop across the river from Derry on the eastern shore – the 'Waterside'.

The city is something of a paradox. The great symbol of Protestant Ulster, it was seized and fortified by Sir Henry Docwra in 1600 as part of the Elizabethan campaign to defeat O'Neill and O'Donnell, the Earls of Tyrone and Tyrconnell who were in arms against the Queen. The Irish Society to whom it was granted in 1613 tried to keep it English and Protestant by sending children over from Christ's Hospital in London to be servants and apprentices and by forbidding the inhabitants from taking Irish apprentices. This was the first of a series of measures to exclude Catholic Irish from Derry; but they kept coming in nonetheless. In 1641 the English and Scottish inhabitants defended the city against the Irish insurgents led by Sir Phelim O'Neill; but the census of 1659 shows 464 Irish in Londonderry, as against 562 English and Scots. The events surrounding the siege of 1689 restored the Protestant character of the city; but in 1808, Wakefield reports:

Londonderry. The town and suburbs contain about 10,000 inhabitants, 1,600 of whom are protestants, and 3,500 catholics: the rest are dissenters. Here the increase of catholics is extraordinary. Some years ago, they were not permitted to live near the place.

It is clear from the various returns made from time to time that, even in the seventeenth century, the main Catholic settlement took place to the west of the city, on the 'bog side' and on the hill of Creggan which rose from the bog, the settlers coming in from Donegal. By the twentieth century the population of Derry was two-thirds Catholic and was concentrated in and around the Bogside area just outside the walls. The symbolic stronghold of Protestantism and loyalism was predominantly Catholic and nationalist. After Partition, Derry became the most notorious example of a Unionist gerrymander. The city ward boundaries were so skilfully drawn, taking in a large part of the Protestant countryside of the county, that the population that was two-thirds nationalist regularly returned in local elections a representation that was two-thirds Unionist.

Like Belfast, Derry was the scene of numbers of nationalist-unionist riots in the nineteenth century. Yet it did not develop the interdenominational bitterness that characterized the Border zone farther south. Perhaps this was because the migration into Derry over long periods had included Presbyterians as well as Catholics, so that its Protestant population wasn't simply one that had stubbornly survived since the Plantation. Perhaps it was because of urbanity. Perhaps it had to do with the particular quality of neighbouring north Donegal, very different from Leitrim, Cavan or Monaghan.

It was in Derry that the current 'Troubles' began, in 1968 and 1969. They derived from a civil rights agitation that concerned primarily the question of discrimination in public housing. The problem then involved has long been solved and forgotten. When the agitation began, the IRA, licking its wounds after the fiasco of the 1950s campaign, had for some years maintained a truce in its 'war' with Britain, a truce that it had unilaterally declared in favour of political demonstrations and mass action. Sinn Féin and the IRA favoured the civil rights agitation of the late 1960s because they saw it as a way towards the revolution they desired, which at this stage was a Marxist revolution. They did not organize it but they gave it their support, supplying chosen volunteers, for example, to act as stewards for the Derry civil rights march of 5 October 1968 which was bloodily stopped by the RUC, and again as protectors of life, if not limb, in the march from Belfast to Derry in January 1969 that was, more bloodily (but without loss of life), stopped by militant loyalists at Burntollet Bridge.

It was in Derry that the full-scale nationalist uprising against the Stormont government began in 1969, when, after youths from the Bogside had stoned the march of the 'Apprentice Boys' and other Orange groups through the city on 12 August (the date which in Derry is the equivalent of 12 July elsewhere in Ulster), the RUC attempted to pursue them back into the Bogside and were met with a resistance that led to three days of street fighting. And it was this episode in turn, with its immediate repercussions in Belfast, that brought about the reinforcement of the British Army in Northern Ireland and its deployment on the streets, and, after a short interval, the resurgence of the IRA.

The Border skirts the suburbs of Derry, a city which is separated from its county by the width of the Foyle and which is bounded on the other three sides by the Republic. Derry is in many ways the chief town of Donegal, or at least of north-east Donegal. Buncrana, a few miles away on the shore of Lough Swilly, serves the city as Dundalk does Newry – as a rest area.

Since 1969 the city has been severely damaged by bombing and then rebuilt and to an extent re-planned. The early reforms that followed the civil rights movement have removed most of the local grievances that exercised nationalists in the 1960s, but these have been replaced by deeper grievances as the nationalists' children enlisted in the Provisional IRA (the Officials in their day had a considerable following in the city, although they carried out several horrific assassinations there) and came into conflict with the British Army, some to die, others to be consigned to the Maze prison at Long Kesh, near Belfast.

Nationalism in Derry before 1969 had expressed itself chiefly in cultural ways – through church, sport, Irish language classes, music and theatre. After 1968 it was a city at war for more than a decade; a new generation has grown up in armed enmity to the United Kingdom. Although the war has diminished, violence flickers on, and nationalist Derry has acquired the attitudes and outlook that must be discussed further in relation to Northern Ireland as a whole.

7

The State of the Republic

The Republic of Ireland is a State created by the Partition of 1921, which was a partition of the United Kingdom, of Ireland and of Ulster. This is an obvious statement of a fact of political history, but it has remained obscure to most of the Republic's citizens. Even those few – Sinn Féin and the IRA – who have consistently pointed out that the State derived from what they describe as a British-imposed partition (and who, therefore, until recently refused to give any recognition to its parliament or its government) did not quite see, or paid no heed to the fact, that a partition of the United Kingdom was also involved. They were not interested in the historic existence of the United Kingdom of Great Britain and Ireland. They were interested in the mythic permanence of the Irish nation which had come down intact from the dawn of history.

A somewhat similar view of the country was held, dimly perhaps, by most of the citizens, but they did not follow the extremist logic of the IRA. The State had been created by the struggle, endurance and determination of their grandparents (give or take a generation) who had fought the British in the period from 1916 to 1922 and had almost achieved the aims of Irish nationalism; had in fact achieved independence for most of Ireland. The State was a worthy and legitimate product of that great endeavour. It wasn't seen as the creation of the British Partition, which was rather a measure of shortfall. *Northern* Ireland was the entity created by Partition. Ireland, as represented by the twenty-six-county State under its successive names, was a country with a bit missing. The ultimate recovery of that missing bit was part of the unfinished business left by the incomplete success of the national struggle.

Ireland's most romantic nationalist hero, Robert Emmet (a man, incidentally, whose intellectual capacity and grasp of political philosophy should not forever remain obscured by his barroom-ballad image), gave nationalism its most romantic expression in the request, made in his speech from the dock when he was condemned to be hanged, drawn and quartered, that his epitaph should not be written until his country took its place 'among the nations of the earth'.

The Irish flag now flies among the other flags at United Nations Plaza in New York, at the administrative headquarters of the European Community in Brussels, at the Olympic Games, wherever they may be held, and at other such places and occasions. But it is very doubtful if that fulfils the condition of Emmet's epitaph. What the flag represents, in terms of international recognition, is not Emmet's Ireland. This is not merely because it is the flag of only a part of the island, but because it represents what any United Irishman of the late eighteenth century would recognize as the largest Irish faction – not the republican Ireland in which the distinctions of Catholic, Protestant and Dissenter had been submerged.

Emmet lived a long time ago, and it would be pointless for people in the present day to feel bound or committed by his (or any other dead hero's) imagining of what was to him the future. But tradition carries a great inertial weight, and political tradition is strong in Ireland. The Irish view of the present – even the view of the young 'global village' generation – is much coloured by past imaginings. Yet, for a country to 'take its place among the nations of the earth' nowadays means something very different from what it meant in Emmet's day.

In 1803, when Emmet was barbarously put to death, nation-states were the supreme autonomous political beings through which liberty could be given full expression. Empires represented the *ancien régime* of a benighted world: the old world of antique despotisms, corrupt accumulations of power and the enslavement of peoples. Both the words, 'empire' and 'nation', had only just begun to be used in a modern sense. The nation, through the French and American examples, was seen as the medium of liberty, the scope or space within which men (and perhaps women – the age is ambiguous on this) could find freedom.

And 'the nations of the earth' was a fairly simple and straightforward concept. The peoples, free of the shackles of superstition and tyranny, would deal with one another on terms of equality, guided by the principles of liberty and benevolence. It is not like that now.

Nearly two hundred years have passed, and we see the world differently, although not necessarily more realistically. Our illusions are simply different from those of the people of 1800. For one thing, we are much more aware of the importance of economics in our lives and to our politics. Or, to tell the truth, we make economics much more important to us. And there are other awarenesses. Adam Smith and Karl Marx, Darwin, Freud and Einstein, to name a significant few, have made it impossible for us to see the world through the eyes of the children of the Enlightenment.

The symbols do not always register such changes. The close-set rank of banners stirring in the breeze off the East River in New York proclaims a world brotherhood of nations, equal in status, united in council, benevolent in purpose. We know that this is not reality; yet in corners of our minds we like to pretend that it is. In other corners perhaps we lazily believe that it is, rather than face the tedium of trying to discover what is reality.

Nation-states are of diminishing importance – although nationalism remains as strong as ever in the world. This may or may not be desirable. It is not clear – if the trend continues – what will replace the autonomous nation-states; whether vast universal (and near-uniform) systems like the USSR and the USA or – since such systems too have their problems with nationalism – something more complex. Perhaps the evolving European Community points the way to the future.

Ireland had, in a way, an advantage in its entry into international life. The Irish Free State of 1922 was not autonomous. Its status was defined within an imperial system. It was a Dominion of the British Empire, on the model of Canada. The acceptance of this status was, of course, bitterly opposed by those who held that their oath to the Irish Republic was permanently binding. This was precisely the issue of the civil war. But it meant that the people who administered Ireland, or that part of it which had an international status, were forced from the beginning to face all the implications, in dealing with other states, of severe limitations of power.

Such limitations cannot be escaped for long anyway; but when

79

they are formally written into treaties and constitutions they are brought home bluntly and coldly to governments. Perhaps Irish governments learned this lesson too well and were a little too timid in their international exercise of their domestic authority. But at least they were enabled to begin their task without undue illusions as to the scope of independence. After the Great War, in the 1920s, when Ireland was one of a number of new or revived nation-states, such illusions were all too possible and were fostered to some extent by the League of Nations. In the 1930s, the realities of power became clearer.

But within the clear and unconcealed limitations, independence had meaning. The British attempt to define Ireland's 'Dominion status', for example, opened up questions about the status of all dominions, especially when it was seen in the context of the much more limited Home Rule Bills of 1886, 1893, 1912 and 1920 – which had been opposed as a threat to the unity of the Empire. (In the Westminster debate on the Anglo-Irish Treaty in December 1921, some speakers, with reason, advised against this definition as unwise.) This gave a chance to the Irish government to play a part in loosening the bonds of Empire, and in gaining thereby an increased scope in international affairs. Ireland played a significant part in the redefinition of the Empire that was embodied in the Statute of Westminster, and it was as a member of the Commonwealth that the State found it possible to remain neutral in the Second World War.

While neutrality demonstrated that independence had real meaning, it showed almost as clearly that limitation of power also continued to be real. The neutral State was dependent for its military supplies on Britain and America, and one side in the War could thereby exercise a direct control over the State's capacity to defend itself should it be invaded. It was necessary for the Irish government at all times to persuade the belligerents that it was not in their interests to infringe Ireland's neutrality; that, at any given moment, the balance of interest lay in respecting it. This was comparable to the diplomacy, largely of implication, which prevented the imposition of military conscription within Northern Ireland, which, as part of the United Kingdom, was technically belligerent, but within which a large part of the population had no commitment to the War and would offer allegiance to the Irish rather than the British State. The calculation was successfully suggested, throughout the six years of war, that the British war effort would benefit more from not imposing conscription on Northern Ireland than from imposing it.

The Irish State was less than twenty years old when the War began in Europe in September 1939. The episode of neutrality was of the greatest importance in the shaping of that State. That Northern Ireland was at war for six years, while the Ireland of twenty-six counties was not, helped to reinforce the distinct twenty-six-county identity that had been mandated by partition. It also raised questions whose answers have still to be worked out. The answers will have an important bearing on future relations between North and South in Ireland and between the Republic, Great Britain and Europe. The Republic, for example, has a very uncertain policy on continued neutrality.

George Washington, in his farewell address to the American people in 1796, on his retirement from his second term in the Presidency, gave some wise advice to the young republic. 'Observe good faith and justice towards all nations', he wrote. 'Cultivate peace and harmony with all. Religion and morality enjoin this conduct. And can it be that good policy does not equally enjoin it? . . .'

> In the execution of such a plan nothing is more essential than that permanent, inveterate antipathies against particular nations and passionate attachments for others should be excluded, and that in place of them just and amicable feelings towards all should be cultivated. The nation which indulges towards another an habitual hatred or an habitual fondness is to some degree a slave. It is a slave to its animosity or to its affections, either of which is sufficient to lead it astray from its duty and its interest . . . There can be no greater error than to expect or calculate upon real favours from nation to nation. It is an illusion which experience must cure, which a just pride ought to discard.

And he went on to advocate a policy of neutrality.

There are people in Ireland who would wish to see such principles applied by the Republic and there are clear indications that a considerable majority of the Republic's citizens favour in some sense a policy of permanent neutrality. But Washington, it must be remembered, had the advantage of presiding over the affairs of a nation which had unequivocally achieved a state of independence and which had the broad Atlantic (a great deal broader, in terms of communications, then than now) to shelter its early development.

The Irish State began in confusion. Throughout the 1920s and the 1930s, after partition and civil war, the achievement of national independence continued to be regarded as unfinished business. Few were thinking seriously about the place in the world at large that a sovereign State of Ireland should occupy. Attention was concentrated on sovereignty itself: on the relationship with Great Britain; and by the time this was more or less resolved (for the twenty-six counties) at the end of the 1930s, the outbreak of the European war, soon to be the World War, had provoked a crisis in which Ireland's international relations had to be improvised in further confusion.

Before this happened, Irish policy in the League of Nations supplies evidence for some support, in international affairs, for principles of nineteenth-century liberalism. There may be here the lingering influence of President Wilson's rhetoric, concerning self-determination and other matters, which had such an appeal in 1918. But there were other reasons for it too. The Cosgrave government of 1922–32 combined an ultramontanist attitude of strict obedience to the Pope and the Catholic bishops in 'matters of faith and morals' – reflecting the views of Pius IX, Cardinal Cullen and the First Vatican Council – with a liberal Catholic tradition that derived from the days of Montalambert and O'Connell. The Fianna Fáil government that succeeded in 1932 was considerably less subservient to bishops and parish priests (who were still, throughout the 1930s, appearing on its opponents' election platforms), but was equally Catholic in its formation – inclining rather more, however, towards what was much later to be known as 'liberation theology'.

The Irish government, in the League, supported the policy of collective security. But the principle of collective security, although it worked in the 1920s in South America and elsewhere, was not applied, in Manchuria or Abyssinia, once major European powers or their interests became involved. The great powers consulted their own interests and went their own way. Éamon de Valera, after he became President of the Executive Council of the Irish Free State and was then elected to the Presidency of the League, made it clear that while Ireland would support genuine collective action by the League against aggression, it saw no reason to be at the behest of the powers as to whether and when action should or should not be taken.

When the Second World War came, Ireland, although a member of the British Commonwealth, was neutral. To this policy, at the time, no alternative was politically possible. Irish membership of the Commonwealth had been imposed, not chosen. Very few people in the State felt any commitment whatever to British imperial policies, in or out of wars, and there was a very large section of the population in 1939 that regarded Britain simply as an enemy not yet fully defeated – still occupying six Irish counties in spite of the expressed will of 'the Irish people'.

Ireland wasn't pitchforked into the War by being attacked, as were Poland, Norway, Denmark, Belgium, the Netherlands, Luxemburg, Albania, Yugoslavia, Greece, the USSR and the USA, among others – all of them neutral up to the point of attack. Nor was there any obvious involvement or imperilment of national interest, such as had brought France and Britain to declare war. Neutrality was both an expression and a test of independence. It showed that Irish sovereignty, by 1939, however limited, was real. But the policy that produced it was very much an *ad hoc* one. There had been no Farewell Address to guide the country (although most of that document would have suited Ireland's situation very well). Guidelines were lacking.

And liberal rationalism went out the window with the Second World War. Auschwitz, Tokyo, Dresden, Hiroshima and Nagasaki introduced us all to an altogether different politics and to the very nasty world in which we now live. The revelations in 1945 of what had gone on in the German-controlled lands during the War – the attempted extermination of Jews, Gypsies and others in Europe by means of mass murder on an unimaginable scale – almost persuaded the Irish that they should have been in the War (as very many of them individually were) on the Allied side. But the corruption of totalitarianism had extended to the Allies too; they too had conducted mass murder – of an admittedly more impersonal kind – in the cities of the nations opposed to them. With the Cold War and its too numerous 'hot' sideshows (such as Vietnam and Afghanistan) there seemed to be a return to ideological conflict on the lines of the futile barbarism of the sixteenth-century wars of religion. The sideshow in Northern Ireland, although much less barbarous than these, is also marked by the moral coarsening that has succeeded the fading of liberal illusions.

In the meantime the Second World War set a precedent for Ireland but can hardly be said to have established a tradition. In the early days of the Cold War, the Irish State, through its politicians, declared itself to be on the side of the West. But, in de Valera's words of 27 September 1951 (replying to a statement of Sir Basil Brooke):

> A partitioned Ireland is not free. An Ireland that is divided and governed in a manner contrary to the wishes of three-fourths of its people must ever have as its first aim the winning back of its unity and independence. Those who partitioned Ireland have pre-determined the attitude of this part of Ireland towards international conflicts in which Britain is a party. Sir Basil Brooke knows this well. Without being false to themselves, those who stand for Ireland can never accept or support as a champion of liberty or democracy, a State whose actions towards Ireland are a denial of both.

Neutrality was again *ad hoc*. Ireland would not join the Atlantic Alliance because the Alliance included Britain and because joining would involve recognizing the borders of the member states, including the Border of Northern Ireland. But, as Ronan Fanning has shown, nationalist Ireland, represented by Sean MacBride in his period as Minister for External Affairs in the government of John A. Costello, was prepared to enter into a bilateral Cold War alliance with the United States.* His proposal was rejected by the United States, which wanted all its European allies to be tidily

---

*Sean MacBride (1904–88): Irish lawyer and international politician. Son of Maud Gonne and Major John MacBride, a leader of 1916 Rising. Chief of Staff of IRA 1936–8. Founder of Clann na Poblachta 1946, which entered coalition government headed by Fine Gael's J. A. Costello.

within the framework of NATO. If it came to war with the Soviet Union, Ireland, as the Americans reasoned, having no significant Communist Party, wouldn't be a problem. It would simply have to fall in with NATO.

Since then, things have changed somewhat. The Treaty of Rome has no military provision; although the move toward closer West-European unity expressed through the Single European Act, has implications for possible military as well as political common action. Ireland is the only country in the Community which is not a member of NATO. Successive Irish governments have maintained the established position on NATO. But Seán Lemass, Jack Lynch, Michael O'Kennedy and Garret FitzGerald, as Ministers for Foreign Affairs or Prime Ministers, have indicated that a 'defence' (for which euphemism read 'war') commitment is implicit in membership of the European Community. Ireland's neutrality, so far, is quite unlike the neutrality of Austria, Switzerland or Sweden.

Since the Second World War, the limitations on independent action have remained clear in the matter of war. The great powers (and, so far as Ireland is concerned, for practical purposes and in respect of major conflict, it is the NATO alliance that really counts) will consult their own interests. Ireland is at the mercy of decisions made elsewhere for reasons which do not relate to it. To join an alliance is to abandon all independence in decision-making on war. To stay out of alliances is to retain some narrow possibility for the government to consult primarily the interests of the Irish people in matters of peace and war. But the possibility will be very narrow indeed.

When the State was founded it wasn't clear to most people that economic independence was no longer possible for a small country. Just before the achievement of independence, at the beginning of the century, nationalist agitation had placed much emphasis on the winning of economic freedom, which was linked, in the propaganda of the time, to political freedom. The government of a free Ireland, it was argued, would place the interests of the Irish people, in economic as in other matters, first.

It seemed for a short time as if this might work. Something on those lines was attempted, initially under the Cumann na nGaedheal government of the 1920s, led by Cosgrave, but notably under the Fianna Fáil governments of the 1930s and 1940s. It was unsuccessful, in spite of the devoted endeavour of the people who built up the 'semi-state' industries of the time, including Aer Lingus, the national airline, the Electricity Supply Board, and the national transport company, Coras Iompair Éireann. In the world we live in, the boundaries of nation states – even the largest of them – are insufficient barriers against the impersonal and supernational operations of the empires of industry and commerce. The systems of finance and production involved are not compatible with such boundaries. In the formation of free trade areas and economic communities these realities have been recognized. Yet the realization is resisted, widely, by almost all the existing nation-states.

Relationships between states are still conducted in ways that are primitive. They were devised in an earlier age and they now relate very inadequately to the reality of power and the character of communications in the contemporary world. For the small and weak state, like Ireland, there are some advantages in this. The failure of correspondence between the formal, or notional, relationships between states and the real relationships, tends often enough to favour the weaker. So, up to a point, Ireland, for example, can carry more than its true weight in the affairs of the European Community, just as small and weak states can in the deliberations of the United Nations Organization – up to a point.

But cunning is needed to work the ju-jitsu trick of applying leverage through weakness. The limitations are set by the tolerance of the strong, and the tolerance of the strong is measured largely in terms of the nuisance-value of the weak. The weak are tempted to fall into two opposed errors: one is to over-reach; the other is to abandon the real value of independence by coming cosily under the wing of a powerful 'partner'.

The State defined by partition, while its governments and people both felt and professed a desire for reunification, went on to discover the reality which conformed to that definition. To quote again, with an added emphasis, de Valera's words to Sir Basil Brooke in 1951: 'Those who partitioned Ireland have pre-determined the attitude of *this part of Ireland* towards international conflicts in which Britain is a party . . .'

The mere fact of having to deal, day by day, with the affairs of 'this part of Ireland' meant that the twenty-six-county unit came to be, not an incomplete Ireland, but a complete entity that functioned – in particular in international relations, but also in many other ways – as a national unit. So, when de Valera came to draft the new Constitution that was passed in 1937, his concern to 'break the connection with England' (in the often quoted words of Tone) wholly overrode any concern with reunification.

The Constitution was passed by and for the population of the twenty-six counties, whatever its first three articles might say about 'the whole island of Ireland'. It was enacted by a slim enough plurality of those who voted in the South but by a minority of the electorates of all Ireland. It reflected an ethos, not the ethos of an Ireland that included all of Ulster, but that of the politically and religiously homogeneous new State. The Constitution was partitionist in that sense and provided a framework within which the population of the *de facto* State could concentrate on establishing its own identity. For many years, however, people in the twenty-six counties could convince themselves that they were candidly open to receive, at some time in the future, the people of the six counties into their State. And the nationalist minority in Northern Ireland thought in the same way.

Things have changed. In the past twenty years the people of the Republic, as the result of the close attention that has been given to all things Northern, have found it necessary to learn about the outlook of people of unionist sentiment in Northern Ireland. This outlook was previously very poorly known or understood in the Republic. Twenty years of debate have adequately filled the gap. Anyone who wanted to know has had ample opportunity to learn what unionists think.

At another level, of course, in those twenty years, a kind of war has been going on in Ireland. It is a war between the IRA and the INLA on the one side, and on the other side the British government and army, with support, sometimes active, from their allies in Ulster. The war is very small-scale and sporadic but it shares with other twentieth-century wars the unpleasant and dangerous feature of having acquired autonomy of purpose. Both sides seem to have lost sight of ultimate political objectives: the ultimate objective is the war.

The war has changed things, not merely in Ulster. Stormont government ended, after half a century, in 1972, brought down partly, it is true, by the civil rights agitation, but partly by the widespread violence that followed the introduction of internment without trial in August 1971. The war also made an impact on the South. There, things had already begun to change drastically. For more than a decade after the end of the Second World War, the Republic, which had successfully maintained its neutrality but economically had barely and with difficulty survived the war, seemed to continue in the old politics and the old ways of the 1920s and 1930s. A frugal self-sufficiency was practised, without great success. There had been much emigration to Britain while the war was on. After a lull, emigration rose again, to exceed 50,000 a year by the middle 1950s – from a population, then, of less than three million. A strict censorship and a general intolerance of dissent from the 'traditional' ways of life of the country (which were in fact mostly no more than a few generations old) still attempted to preserve Ireland from the infidel world of the twentieth century.

The great break came about 1960. We may take the elevation of Éamon de Valera from leadership in party politics to the Presidency in 1959 to be the symbolic event. The symbols, myth and aspirations of the nationalist past were not officially discarded. They remained part of the rhetorical stock-in-trade. But the State in effect took a new direction and turned its back on them. The country, with the first and second 'Programmes for Economic Expansion' (beginning in 1958), went into a period of boom. Ireland, along with the United Kingdom and Denmark, joined the European Common Market, at the beginning of 1973. That, however, was to be the year of the Yom Kippur War and of the ensuing oil crisis. After a period of economic instability, during which Irish farming received considerable hand-out benefit from Brussels, things deteriorated badly in the 1980s. The country went into a period of bust.

From the early 1960s the kinds of people who are nowadays labelled 'yuppies' became conspicuous in the Republic as elsewhere: brash, ignorant, thrusting and mundanely ambitious, knowledgeable in business and some other techniques and in very little else, consumers of trivia, trendy and shallow. They helped produce both the boom and the bust. They did much both to turn the country from its nationalist ideas and preoccupations of the previous century or so and also to abandon irredentism and to accept, not merely pragmatically and reluctantly, but quite comfortably, a twenty-six-county identity.

This caused a slowly spreading bewilderment, especially in rural Ireland, the chief base of traditional nationalism. But the culture of rural Ireland, of the old style, had been mortally wounded by the mass emigration of the preceding decades. The Republic, by the 1970s, was suddenly an urban society, with a growing population. By the later 1970s half of that population was under twenty-five years of age. Then, as economic depression set in, and with it unemployment, the State went into social and economic crisis. The young population began to leave the country in growing numbers, to go to Britain in spite of the growing unemployment there, or to go to America, in spite of the restrictions there on immigration from Europe.

It is interesting but not very useful to speculate on the influence the developments in Northern Ireland had on all this. On the North too, external events made their impact. Ireland is, notoriously, a conservative country; but one of the things that strikes the observant visitor from the South is the archaism – in some respects – of the North.

Northern Ireland was so locked into a late-nineteenth-century social and political configuration by the undying issue of the Union that when change came, it shattered the structure. Before the eyes of people in the South there occurred something comparable in a way to the 1916 Rising, but it happened in Derry and Belfast. This caused the utmost confusion in the Republic.

In the first place, what was still then (in 1969) an official and widespread ideology called for sympathy for the cause of the nationalist uprising in the North, and therefore for some measure of support for it. But the Northerners had acted autonomously. They hadn't waited, as was their assigned role, for a lead from Dublin. And, initially at any rate, they had indicated that they could go it alone: they did not need or want help from Dublin. By the time that position changed, other issues besides civil rights had come to the surface. The confusion in the Republic increased. Was the tail trying to wag the dog? There was, after all, an Irish State, an Irish government. The northern insurgents were believed to aspire to a united Ireland. Shouldn't they, then, take their lead from the Irish government, which, if it was not exactly the government of a united Ireland, was legitimately elected by the people of unoccupied Ireland and was best entitled to speak and act for the people of all Ireland?

When the IRA attempted to take over the leadership of the nationalist cause in the North, the position became at once clearer and more difficult. The IRA did not recognize the Dublin government as legitimate. The Dublin government did not recognize the IRA as legitimate. The Dublin government did, on the other hand, recognize the constitutional political movement which had in fact preceded the IRA in leadership of the uprising of the late 1960s – in its non-violent and most successful phase. That movement in due course took shape as the SDLP.

But this meant, for the Dublin government, giving a recognition that had hitherto been carefully avoided, that is, to some legitimacy for British rule in the North. Éamon de Valera, for example, had been scrupulously careful, in all his dealings that involved this issue, to maintain the *de jure* claim to all Ireland that is embodied in the first three articles of the Constitution. Now, forced by the Northern uprising to take some position, the government in the Republic was associating itself with the supplicant politics of a subordinate within the British system. This contradiction for a long time paralysed the government.

The contradiction reflects, accurately enough, the confusion that ensued after the beginning of the Northern insurrection. In effect, the national identity perceived by the government in Dublin is that of the existing twenty-six-county State: this is the polity they deal with and represent day to day and it has been a distinct entity for two-thirds of a century. To a large extent such a sense of the State is shared by the citizens of the Republic. The aspiration to a united Ireland was both real and unreal. Most of the politicians down the years genuinely thought it would be a good thing to have. But they consistently took actions that led in another direction.

This led to a primary contradiction. Because of its broad commitment to a united Ireland and in particular because of the *de jure* claim, Irish policy had undertaken certain responsibilities in respect of Northern Ireland. Persons born in Northern Ireland, for example, were and are entitled to Irish citizenship as if they had been born in the Republic. During the Second World War, when the Germans bombed Belfast, de Valera both sent immediate help northwards in the form of firefighting and other emergency services, and afterwards protested formally to the German government. When the Americans staged some of their troops in Northern Ireland before the Normandy landings, de Valera formally protested because they had done this without his government's consent. And in many other ways in international dealings – not least in the long refusal to make a commitment to any instrument or organization that required the recognition of existing boundaries, including the Border – Irish policy had conformed strictly to the sense of the Constitution.

The Dublin government at the end of the 1960s could not, therefore, say to the British: 'Northern Ireland is British; it's your mess; you handle it.' On the other hand, because it recognized Britain's *de facto* position both in theory (including the Constitution) and in long practice, it could not say: 'Northern Ireland is ours: you have no business to be there and you'll receive no cooperation from us to hold it down: get out; we'll handle it.'

A Dublin government made its own contribution to the Northern upheaval of the late 1960s. Seán Lemass, who had succeeded Éamon de Valera as Taoiseach in 1959, said of Northern Ireland in a speech in 1963 that: 'We recognize that the Government and Parliament there exist with the support of the majority of the people of the Six County area – artificial though that area is . . .' And he went on to renew de Valera's proposal of 1938, that Stormont, after reunification, should retain its devolved powers, but under an all-Ireland rather than the United Kingdom parliament. His emphasis was notably different from de Valera's: it proposed in effect a direct dealing with the Northern unionists. As he put it: 'The solution of the problem of partition is one to be found in Ireland by Irishmen . . .'

The Irish State had been cooperating with Northern Ireland and its government, since shortly after the War, in some economic matters, including drainage, hydroelectricity and fisheries along the

Border, and joint governmental management of the railway linking Dublin and Belfast. Early in 1965, Lemass, without prior public announcement, went to Belfast to confer with the Stormont Prime Minister, then Captain Terence O'Neill. This was the first meeting of the Dublin and Stormont prime ministers since the period of partition. The meeting was soon followed by a return visit of Captain O'Neill to Dublin.

Captain O'Neill had already been making some effort to loosen the rigid political structure of Northern Ireland – a dangerous process, since fear of any political change had become a major part of unionism. Like Lemass, he was, among other things, looking forward to the new situation that would be created by membership of the European Communities, for which both Britain and Ireland had recently applied. Now – in the eyes of the more extreme loyalists – he was supping with the devil but using a short spoon. The growing cooperation between Dublin and Belfast, joined to the growing pressure for equal rights in practice as well as law for Catholics in Northern Ireland, led to an increase in tension there.

But there was a political rigidity in the South too, not so much in day-to-day politics as in the insufficiently examined 'national aspirations'; the general acceptance of the view that there were tasks of nation-building yet to be completed, including in particular the revival of the Irish language and the 'reunification of the national territory'. It is to be noted that this was the phrase commonly used: 'reunification of the national *territory*'. Lemass was beginning to move in a somewhat different direction – towards a unification of people. It is fairly certain that this was his ultimate objective, but his immediate purpose was concerned more with the practicalities of day-to-day politics. He was replaced as Taoiseach by Jack Lynch, of Cork, who had stepped in as the compromise candidate when there was a bitter contest for the leadership of the Fianna Fáil party between Lemass's son-in-law Charles Haughey and Haughey's schoolmate George Colley. Lynch was head of the government and leader of a somewhat divided party when the upheaval began in the North.

Fianna Fáil, in government from 1932 to 1948, from 1951 to 1954, and now since 1957, represented a section of the republicans who had been defeated in the civil war of 1922–1923. It called itself 'the Republican Party', and it made much show of its devotion to the 'national aspirations', although in recent years it had abandoned the attempted self-sufficiency of de Valera's policies and was engaged in efforts to modernize Ireland's economy in accordance with the developments of Western (especially European) capitalism. The party had long regarded itself as the patron and friend of Northern nationalism.

When the civil rights movement in Northern Ireland caused such turmoil at the end of the 1960s, the Fianna Fáil party, in government in Dublin, was itself thrown into some disarray. Some of its leading members, ministers of government, saw one of the party's long-term aims come suddenly within sight: there was a civil uprising against the British-backed regime in the North. Simultaneously they saw a client population acting on its own without reference to its Southern mentor. The impulse to intervene was very strong; both to retain Fianna Fáil leadership of Northern nationalism and to support what was seen as a justified rebellion.

The widespread fighting, in Derry and Belfast, in 1969, which led to a number of deaths and to the entry of the British Army (initially in a pacific demeanour) into the conflict, provoked a crisis in the Dublin government. Some ministers wanted Southern military intervention – at least to the extent of sending soldiers across the Border two or three miles into Derry's Bogside. Some were inclined to help the Northern nationalists in other ways – by supplying them with anything from propaganda to arms.

The government, like the Stormont government and the British government, was taken by surprise by what had happened. In spite of the many speeches made by politicians about reunification, no preparations for such an event had been made. Propaganda on reunification had been directed against Britain, on the grounds that Britain had partitioned Ireland unjustly and it was therefore up to Britain to undo this wrong. But Northern Ireland affairs, being, according to the official ideology, a domestic matter, could not therefore be within the scope of activity of the Department of External Affairs (as it then was) but were assigned to the Department of the Taoiseach. By a delightfully ironic application of the doublethink which pervaded these matters they were then *seconded* to the Department of External Affairs; but interest in

Northern Ireland was not active enough to justify the full-time attention of even one senior officer there.

Information was therefore poor, and such policy as had been formulated was irrelevant to what was now happening. Public opinion in the Republic reacted to the events of 1968–1972 in waves of sympathy with what it saw as the righteous cause of the oppressed (the Catholic nationalists) in the North. Jack Lynch, whose career had been remote from the North and its concerns and whose personal background was not that of traditionalist Fianna Fáil republicanism, had to placate an inflamed public opinion, restrain those of his colleagues whose impulse was to intervene in one way or another in the North, and to cobble together a policy. He handled public opinion at moments of high excitement by issuing carefully crafted statements that sounded much more bold, firm and belligerent than their content justified when critically read. Things got out of control once, in the immediate aftermath of 'Bloody Sunday' – 30 January 1972, when British parachute troops shot and killed thirteen unarmed men and youths on the occasion of a large civil rights march in Derry. The Irish government was well represented at the funerals; Lynch declared a day of national mourning in the Republic, and a huge crowd on that day marched on the British embassy in Dublin. A section of the crowd firebombed the embassy and burned it to the ground. That led to a recall of ambassadors. The British applied severe pressures of various kinds to the Republic. Tourism – a major business in Ireland – was sharply affected. Numerous Anglo-Irish sports meetings were cancelled. People in all parts of the Republic began to realize that what was happening in the North could have direct and sometimes serious effects on them.

And, meantime, the emphasis in the North shifted from peaceful agitation for civil rights to a new politics and to a renewal of the old conspiratorial and insurrectionary nationalism. The IRA, caught off balance as much as anyone else by the explosion of 1969, held a meeting of the 'Army Council' in December of that year, at which there were bitter recriminations (coming chiefly from the Northerners). The policy of disarmament in favour of disruptive agitation on matters such as housing and fishing rights was blamed for the IRA's failure in one of its traditional roles in Belfast in August, when it was

94

unable to defend the Catholic streets in the Falls area. The dissidents – mostly Northerners – walked out of this meeting and set up a 'provisional Army Council', while the – mostly Marxist – supporters of the policy of politicization remained, as the 'official Army Council'. This split was repeated at the general meeting of the Sinn Féin party in January 1970.

Both the 'Provisional IRA' and the 'Official IRA' moved into violent action in 1970 and 1971. At the beginning many people in the South found it easy to sympathize with them: weren't they, after all, resuming the fight that had secured independence for most of Ireland half a century earlier? But the violence soon took a turn that made it unacceptable. And the changes that rapidly took place in Northern politics soon made Northern Ireland appear more and more inexplicable and alien to people in the South.

Oddly enough, the fall of Stormont and the reimposition of direct British rule in 1972 marked the point at which public opinion in the Republic began slowly to veer. The change revealed a deep underlying structure in Irish nationalism. Its primary motivation had always arisen from the local: the sense of immediate oppression, exercised as it had been for generations in Ireland by a privileged, legally exclusive, caste of Protestants, behind whom stood the power of Great Britain. It is common for the oppressed to blame not the king but his advisers; so, in Ireland, there had long been the custom of supplicating the superior imperial power to mitigate the excesses of the local, immediate, tyrant. Now, Irish opinion turned with some relief to direct dealings with the British, who seemed to have done Northern Ireland the service of removing the Orange boot from the neck of the suffering Gael. Even within Northern Ireland, in August 1969, the advent of the British Army on the streets had been greeted by nationalists – suddenly relieved from the onslaughts of the RUC, including the hated B-Specials, who had just been brought in to the aid of the exhausted regular constabulary – with gestures of welcome, including offers of cups of tea.

A great deal has been read, mistakenly, into these cups of tea. Both Irish sides – the Stormont government and its forces, and the nationalist populations of Derry and Belfast – had been exhausted by the confrontations of the week. The people of the Bogside and

Creggan in Derry thought that they had won a defensive victory. The British troops who suddenly appeared, unlike the RUC whom they replaced, did not immediately try to move in to the areas that had been defended with petrol bombs. That their ultimate objective was to succeed where the RUC had failed and to put down an uprising was as yet far from clear. When the Home Secretary, James Callaghan, flew over from London, went into the Bogside and left the people with the impression that he supported them against the tyranny of Stormont, they were fully misled in their understanding of what had just happened. In fact, a system that had failed for fifty years was being replaced by a system that had failed for five hundred years.

From this point on Southern opinion moved, very slowly perhaps, but very steadily, away from sympathy with the nationalists of the North, or at least from sympathy with the militant nationalists who employed the bomb and the gun. And the Irish government began constructing a policy which involved fairly close consultation with the British and a rather more than merely *de facto* recognition of Great Britain's position in Northern Ireland; a renunciation of military or violent means to solve the problem; a continued long-term aspiration to a united Ireland; a short-term aim of stabilizing Northern Ireland (and the Republic) by opposing the IRA and its agnates and by acting, in relation to the British government on behalf of the nationalists of Northern Ireland, as 'the second guarantor' (to borrow Jack Lynch's words of 1969) – pressing the British to restrain the unionists.

Opinion fluctuates, and polls are of small value to gauge it, although they have some. On such a subject as Northern Ireland, most people in the Republic are not sure what they think: the situation is most confusing. The nature of the war is such that it seems to consist almost wholly of atrocities – on both sides – with little of the heroics that are part of the public relations of conventional wars. Only one side in practice has control of propaganda on the mass media. This is highly effective outside Ireland (where the conflict is regularly presented as simply a religious war between Protestants and Catholics with the British government doing its best to keep peace between them). In Ireland this control is partly, but only partly, vitiated by the availability of other sources of information close to hand. And in Ireland this information is confusing.

In looking at the public in the South it is necessary to make distinctions. There are what we might call the 'pre-1959' people, those who were mature and active in life and politics in the days when the traditional nationalist outlook still dominated. Such people are now a minority, but are of importance still because they include the principal political leaders. The leaders are important because they still make decisions. But they do not really lead: their importance is ephemeral. The leaders of the Fianna Fáil, Fine Gael and Labour parties have nothing like the command over their followers that their predecessors had a generation earlier – although Charles Haughey perhaps has that command over a section of Fianna Fáil.

Then there are the people in their late twenties, thirties and early forties. In any country people of this age are the most important if we are trying to look ten or fifteen years ahead. Not everyone in the age-group, perhaps; but those who are articulate, active and in positions to control and influence events – many of them already beginning to lead in various fields. Here there is much less of the old nationalism (such as is preserved in amber in the North) and little of the sense of national identity founded on the old myth. This is a cohort born two generations after independence. They have a sense of national identity which is just that: a sense, not a conscious working out. 'We're here because we're here because we're here.' Some of them are implicated in the decisions that have run the country into its present economic mess. There is developing among this group a lively and radical criticism of the present state of things. But Ireland is in many (not all) matters a conservative country. It sniffed at, but did not accept, the Marxist remedies now slowly fading in appeal but once offering a cure for all the country's ills. Happily, it will probably be as slow to accept the extremist capitalist ideologies suddenly in fashion in their place. The young-middle aged generation in Ireland is pragmatic, and largely liberal.

Then there are those under twenty-five – half the population until large numbers of them began to leave just a few years ago. Here it becomes more difficult to diagnose. Almost by definition, these have not made their mark yet (in contrast to their fellows in

Northern Ireland, who have been thoroughly politicized and some of whom by now are well into their life-sentences in Long Kesh).

There are some pointers. An important one was the 1983 referendum to amend the Constitution by writing into it an absolute prohibition on abortion. The then leaders of the two main political parties, Charles Haughey and Garret FitzGerald, followed parallel lines of least resistance, and the campaign was conducted largely by agitational groups. It provided a rare test in which the Roman Catholic Church – after much hesitation – tried its strength against forces of change. The Church won a handsome but possibly a pyrrhic victory. The Church-supported amendment won by two-to-one of the popular vote. But the poll was very low for an Irish election – around fifty per cent. The vote in urban middle-class constituencies was two-to-one against. In urban working-class constituencies it was about two-to-one for. In rural areas it was five-or six-to-one for. If we bear in mind that Ireland is an urbanizing country and that this is the single most favourable issue that the Church could have chosen to fight on – in Ireland or elsewhere – the result can only be seen as an indicator of profound change.

A less clear pointer is provided by the 1986 referendum on divorce. Article 41.3.2 of the Constitution states that: 'No law shall be enacted providing for the grant of a dissolution of marriage.' Recent polls, taken both before and after the referendum have shown that the public is in favour, by a margin of 60:40, of permitting divorce in some circumstances. When the FitzGerald government, however, introduced a referendum bill on this matter, instead of proposing simply that Article 41.3.2 should be deleted, leaving it to the legislature to introduce, debate and amend as necessary any legislation introducing divorce, it tried to hedge against criticism by attempting to introduce a complicated and cautious piece of legislation into the Constitution. The opponents of divorce seized on the flaws in this and tore it to shreds, persuading a large part of the electorate that it embodied a serious threat to the property rights of the 'first family' in divorce cases. Pusillanimity combined with a piece of dubious (and very bad) draughting, and the opportunism of Fianna Fáil (then in opposition) to create confusion and consolidate the Catholic character of the Constitution.

The two referendums appear to show that nothing changes. But change happens. North and South, Ireland is a victim of the fashionable ideologies that produce crushing unemployment. Irish identity is neither in doubt nor a subject of much interest or speculation among young people. On the other hand they are keenly interested in their own society. Irish people read nowadays – more than other Europeans (except Icelanders). And they read about the world they live in. In the large shopping centres there are bookshops. In every bookshop there is a large section of books of Irish interest. In such sections the books are very numerous. This is one indicator. The arts flourish, in an economically deeply depressed country. Some adaptation is occurring, to what we might soon, perhaps, begin to call the post-industrial world. Exports are booming. Those large numbers of young people who have been thronging to Boston or London are much better educated than their predecessors of earlier emigrations and bring with them a quite different kind of nostalgia for their homeland. Some return. The future, leaving the North aside, is uncertain but not wholly unhopeful.

The North cannot be left aside; but on that problem there can be quite varied views, in quarters that might be lumped together as nationalist. For increasing numbers of Irish people, the Ulster problem is moving right out of the old framework of nationalist thought. That does not mean that it is moving out of their minds. These are comparatively open.

8

Ulster Will Be Right

The province, or sub-province, which came to be known as 'Northern Ireland' was based indirectly on a political reality: that most Irish Protestants had come to be strongly opposed to Dublin Home Rule and that there was a concentration of Protestants in north-eastern Ireland, forming in places large local majorities.

In one way the opposition that gave rise to partition goes back to the days of the seventeenth-century migrations. Since that date, many Protestants in Ireland have feared, and have been prepared to resist, Catholic government, partly on religious grounds, partly on political. Besides having an abhorrence of Catholic teachings and associating Popery with tyranny and absolutism, they knew by the end of the seventeenth century that almost all Protestant property, power and privilege in Ireland had been confiscated from Catholics: Catholics therefore formed a powerful and dangerous reversionary interest.

This continuity has been obscured by some developments which have caused confusion to nationalists. Protestantism in Ireland has never been homogeneous, and in particular there has always been a sharp distinction between two large groups, both very numerous in Ulster, the Presbyterians and the Anglicans (who fairly regularly appear as 'Scotch' and 'English' in seventeenth- and eighteenth-century enumerations; otherwise as 'dissenters' and 'protestants'). Within Presbyterianism there was a distinction between the 'New Light' and the 'Old Light'. The New Light Presbyterians tended towards a Whiggish politics. The others tended towards a political Toryism.

Orangeism was, broadly, Tory, and initially largely Anglican, although from the beginning there were some Presbyterian tenant farmers involved. People of this persuasion feared Roman

Catholicism as such and saw in it a creed devoted to the destruction of Protestantism and in particular of the Protestant settlement in Ulster. Their view, almost in its seventeenth-century form, has been consistently expressed in recent times by Rev. Ian Paisley, not so much in his broader political pronouncements as in his religious pamphlets and sermons and in the pages of the virulent paper he published for a number of years, the *Protestant Telegraph*.

The Whiggish, or liberal, view held by New Light Presbyterians and some others was centred on Belfast in the late eighteenth century. It aligned fairly easily with the views of eighteenth-century deists, especially in being comparatively free of fear of Catholics. It was a view that readily accommodated the republican ideas formulated by the societies of United Irishmen at the end of the century, who were the first to aim at an Irish republic separate from Britain.

This is what has caused the nationalist confusion that still persists in the historical perceptions of, for example, Sinn Féin. For nationalist history taught that there was a golden age at the end of the eighteenth century when 'Catholic, Protestant and Dissenter' united in 'the common name of Irishman' to 'break the connection with England' and set up an independent Irish republic (the phrases quoted are all from Tone, but out of context). It has led to much misunderstanding of Ulster unionism. It is quite possible for an Ulsterman to be proud of his United Irish ancestor who fought or was hanged in '98 and still to be a unionist.

For what the United Irishmen aimed at was a republic; and a republic at the end of the eighteenth century was a secular state. Far from proposing a revival of the old aristocratic Catholic Ireland of the 'Wild Geese' that offered its loyalty to the Stuarts, they proposed a wholly new Ireland in which the various creeds and denominations would be unimportant as distinctions partly because they were unimportant in themselves: old prejudices and super-stitions would carry no weight under enlightened government; old cultural traditions would give way to the rational state.

All of this perished in the horrors of 1798. The government, through remarkable good luck (as in the storms that scattered the French expedition of 1796) and through its successful penetration of the United Irish societies with spies and *agents provocateurs*,

101

scotched the revolutionary organization; but through its brutal repression of the widespread support for rebellion among the people it helped provoke a series of uprisings around the country. In Antrim and Down 'the people' (their own term for their cause) – mostly Presbyterians but including Anglicans and some Catholics – rose against the government. In Wexford and elsewhere the people rose against their immediate oppressors, the whole rural and small-town élite, whom they identified readily enough by the badge of religion (the 'Popery Laws' had already established religion as the distinction between the privileged and the excluded), seeking out Protestants, to pike them to death on the bridge at Wexford, to burn men, women and children in a barn at Scullabogue, as well as staunchly fighting the professional and the part-time soldiers of the Crown.

And there was a revival of religion at the beginning of the new century, to be followed, notably in Ulster, by several further revivals. The aspiration to a secular state and the apotheosis of Reason in place of the Old Testament God, gave way to religious enthusiasm, while an outlook wholly different from eighteenth-century deism prevailed among those who ruled and administered the nations of Europe.

Ulster Protestant liberalism survived all this, but after 1800 was comfortable enough within the Union, which was a safeguard from the horrors of Catholic jacqueries and also gave opportunity for political reform within a United Kingdom that could encompass an Irish personality – as well as an English, a Scottish and a Welsh – and that offered a place to Ulster under the aegis of the great liberalizing and modernizing world power. The liberals regarded themselves as Irish, but they drifted steadily away from the nationalists. They took quite a keen interest in the culture and traditions of their native land; but this was not the mainspring of their politics. They could, for example, enjoy the sentimental ballads and *Irish Melodies* of Tom Moore, with their inbuilt lament for the vanished glories of ancient Ireland*; they could appreciate the old tradition of harp music, which survived in Ulster well into the nineteenth century after it had died away elsewhere; they could

---

*Tom Moore (1779–1852): best-selling poet and friend of Byron, author of 'The Minstral Boy', 'The Harp That Once' and *Lalla Rookh*.

take a benevolent interest in the Irish language and its literature and in the Irish history that preceded the Plantation; but their politics derived from a general liberalizing tendency within the United Kingdom as a whole. The more extravagant manifestations of Catholic nationalism did not appeal to them, and they certainly could only look with unease upon the great Repeal of the Union campaign organized by O'Connell, with the peasant masses at his back and his cohorts of priest lieutenants by his side. And the violence of rural secret societies, which was to mesh more and more as the century wore on with separatist nationalist organizations and revolutionary conspiracies: that held no appeal whatever for them.

The period between O'Connell's achievement of Catholic Emancipation in 1829 and the final vast mass meetings of his Repeal campaign in the early 1840s saw a regrouping within Protestant Ulster that foreshadowed the unionist solidarity of a generation later. The Emancipation agitation had given rise to very bitter and often very bigoted controversy; but on this matter Protestant opinion was divided. Nobody who subscribed in any appreciable measure to the liberal ideas of the nineteenth century – nobody who was 'progressive' in supporting the growth of industry, the freeing of trade, the widening of the franchise, the extension of education to the masses, and the rational ordering of political, social and economic affairs – could be other than disquieted at the exclusion of Catholics (and Jews) from full participation in the political and social life of the Kingdom. It was the Tory and Orange party that bitterly opposed Emancipation, fearful as it was of Roman Catholicism, which it saw as a foreign and obscurantist religion. The Orange view also saw it as a conspiracy to destroy the 'freedom, religion and laws' of the United Kingdom – but in particular of Ireland where the Catholic evil was already so deeply rooted. The great force that O'Connell was able to summon to his support, acting on the divided Protestant opinion as reflected in Parliament, enabled Emancipation to pass.

Repeal of the Union was a different matter. No simple appeal to liberal principles could be made on its behalf. A right to national self-determination was widely acknowledged, it is true; and the middle of the nineteenth century was perhaps the time when plebiscitary votes were held in the highest moral esteem among

European liberals. But romantic nationalism didn't quite square with liberal principles. What had the greatest appeal for liberals was a political system which best guaranteed the liberty and prosperity of the individuals within it; and to liberal Protestants in Ireland at about 1840 this must have seemed to be offered much more securely by the United Kingdom – which was visibly on the path of progress – than by the O'Connellites, lay and clerical, whose sought-after Kingdom of Ireland, run by them, could well be envisaged as an Irish version of the Papal States where, in 1840, there were bans in force not only on liberal principles and a free press, but on railways too.

O'Connell had tried unsuccessfully to carry north his campaign for Catholic Emancipation, having first made a series of speeches attacking Orangeism. The Orange Order organized parades, mass meetings and other displays at which Catholicism was denounced; a highly sensationalist history was confected of Protestant Ulster since the Plantation and was conveyed through all available media to the Protestant masses in Ulster; and the Emancipation campaign was portrayed as a prelude to a rebellion in which the horrors of 1641 and 1798 would be re-enacted and fire and sword would be loosed on the province. A march to promote Emancipation, led north from Dublin by the Belfastman John Lawless, was treated as if it were a foreign invasion of Ulster, was met by armed Orangemen in Co. Monaghan and was stopped at Armagh.

In 1836 the government banned the Orange Order because of the factionalism it provoked and the dangerous violence associated with its meetings and parades. But in 1841, when O'Connell himself tried to bring his Repeal agitation to the North, he was met with such determined and coordinated resistance that his attempted meeting in Belfast was a fiasco. This visit too was portrayed as an invasion of Ulster in subsequent speeches by Rev. Henry Cooke, the Presbyterian minister whose voice was the most powerful and strident in support of the Union and who had already gone a long way towards bringing Presbyterians and Anglicans together politically in its defence. A moral border was drawn and was fairly successfully defended by the Ulster unionists of the day.

Protestant religious fanaticism was bolstered by the common-sense views of businessmen, many of them liberal in their political outlook, who could point to the prospering manufactures of the Belfast area, which they attributed to the Union and to the ready accessibility of the open British market. The rest of Ireland had not prospered under the Union, but this was attributed not to the Union but to the inferior discipline, habits and attitudes of the Catholic Irish.

The Repeal campaign ended with the government banning of the monster meeting O'Connell had announced for Clontarf, on the outskirts of Dublin, in 1843. The venue had been chosen partly for its symbolism (but also to bring half a million people or more within shouting distance of the seat of British government in Ireland). It was there, in 1014, that the High King Brian Boru had won a battle which romantic history in the nineteenth century portrayed as a victory that had freed Ireland from the foreign yoke of the Danes. But O'Connell won no victory there. His gathering multitude dispersed and the campaign to break the Union was over.

Within a few years very large changes came over Ireland, including Ulster. The great Famine of the 1840s is one of the most significant divides in modern Irish history. A population that had doubled in half a century to well over eight million began to decline, probably just before the Famine; and with the Famine the decline became very rapid. The disaster was most terrible in western parts of the island, and displacement of people occurred in three ways. Many died, many left Ireland, many thronged from the devastated to more prosperous parts of the country. In west Ulster some parishes lost more than half their people through death from starvation and 'famine fever'. Survivors, some of them, fled to the east, where the visitation had been much less severe. Catholics in large numbers began to arrive in some areas that had been overwhelmingly Protestant for almost two hundred years –notably Belfast. That city was growing very fast already as its manufactures increased; and in the decades just after the Famine it added new industries – engineering and shipbuilding – and drew in more people – skilled and semi-skilled workers from Britain (in particular Scotland) and unskilled workers, both Protestant and Catholic, from rural Ulster. On a smaller scale something similar happened in Derry.

Poor Catholics crowding into cities that could not expand fast enough to accommodate burgeoning populations, intruding on areas where the established way of life and outlook were Protestant, engendered and encountered hostility. Protestant-Catholic riots were already a feature of life among the labouring classes in Ulster, since tension and hostility had been aroused by the Emancipation and Repeal agitations. Older tension and hostility were imported by migrants from south Ulster, where there had been rural conflict between Catholics and Protestants competing both for land and for putting-out work since the second half of the eighteenth century. Recurring riots continued, on a larger scale, and began to take on a fairly straightforward political character by the 1880s: for or against the Union or Home Rule.

The 'mechanics' and other skilled and semi-skilled workers in the fast-expanding industries of the North, not to speak of the urban labourers and those of rural origin and prejudice, could find nothing in common, in their situation or outlook, with the tenant-farmers of Connacht and Munster, and little, for that matter, in common with the shop-assistants and schoolmasters of those provinces. Everything in their religious background tended to prejudice them against Catholics; while their social and economic status within a modernizing society linked them to their fellows on Clydeside and Tyneside or in Lancashire or the Black Country, but separated them from working people in a decayed rural traditional society – which is what much of Ireland was in the decline of Ascendancy landlordism. The powerful impact of fundamentalist revivalism in Belfast just after the turn of the century tended, it is true, to set a large section of the sectarian-Protestant working people apart from their church-Protestant 'betters' in Ulster – and this reinforced a class distinction which remains important still – but, even more, it set them apart from Roman Catholics. It also reinforced the imperialist instincts of the lumpen proletariat – instincts which played a part in the political conflict of 1886–1912. To the present day, on the banners of loyalist Ulster, Queen Victoria hands the Bible to the grateful hands of kneeling black African children, and Ulster loyalists have an instinctive sympathy and fellow feeling with the white government of South Africa.

A. T. Q. Stewart, in *The Narrow Ground*, and David Miller, in *The Queen's Rebels*, have both written very perceptively about the particular character of Ulster Presbyterianism. David Miller has shown, for example, the importance of the Scottish tradition of 'public banding' for the ways in which Ulster Protestants have organized themselves to meet the emergencies of the politics of Home Rule and the Union. A. T. Q. Stewart has related the habits and attitudes of the Kirk to the politics of the Presbyterians, 'besieged' by the Irish Catholics. But there is a little more to be said. For the 'siege' has had a deleterious effect over the years on Ulster Presbyterianism. Liberalism, an essential leaven for the Presbyterian spirit, has been all but discarded. The debate, theological, philosophical and political, which characterized the Presbyterianism of the eighteenth and early nineteenth centuries has given way to a conformity enforced by the fear that any deviation from a hard line (in particular any political deviation) may lead to a betrayal of the cause to the enemy without the gates. It is almost impossible nowadays for a liberal minister, but particularly a radical minister, to receive a call; or, if by chance he receives it, to retain the confidence of his congregation. In the end, a church that once had a great deal to say to the larger community of which it is a part, has nothing to say. Orangeism, from the mid-nineteenth century onwards, so far as politics is concerned, gradually swallowed up Presbyterianism in Ulster. Oddly enough, nowadays it is the Church of Ireland that is more open to treat with the Irish majority on reasonable terms; although the experience of the late Bishop Hanson in his short term in the Diocese of Clogher shows that there are very considerable difficulties there too.

It must be remembered too that apart from Presbyterians and Anglicans there are many other Protestants in Northern Ireland, including, for example, Methodists, Baptists, Dr Paisley's Free Presbyterians, and smaller sects. 'Born again' Christians are numerous in all groups, and there are many Protestants who rejoice in the certainty that they are saved while finding consolation or regret, according to their inclination, in the knowledge that most of their fellow Protestants (not to speak of Catholics) are damned to hellfire for all eternity. This kind of inside information has helped to make life interesting for large numbers of people even in the drabbest of surroundings since the Reformation.

In the light of such melodrama, played out against the background of eternity, temporal politics may seem a small matter. But justification, like the love of praise or money, feeds on excess. The elect take a lively view of their earthly circumstances, surrounded as they are by the reprobate, and this can find expression in political as much as in religious enthusiasms. As E. Estyn Evans put it in his pamphlet *The Common Ground* (1984),

> . . .One of the most alarming facts about Ulster – and here I quote a Methodist minister – is that it contains the most notorious Bible belt in Protestantism. Now I would disagree only in one way: there is an even more notorious Bible belt in the heart of the eastern United States of America, in Kentucky and Tennessee, to which, historically, the Presbyterian emigrants of Ulster made a baneful contribution. Fundamentalism, and Evangelicalism I regard as blind and dangerous forces. I'm a pagan, quite frankly. But the extreme Presbyterians have no monopoly of absolutist doctrines, and I think that is near the root of our problem.

Much of the Bible belt is rural, and it too is quite complex; for there are places where unreconstructed seventeenth-century fundamentalism survives, as in parts of north-eastern County Down, while there are more numerous small groups derived from Evangelical enthusiasms generated by the dislocations and dis-orientations caused by nineteenth-century industrialization, or by the subsequent failures of industries.

Eastern Ulster took part in the final developments of the first phase of the Industrial Revolution, and in the second, railway – and steamship – building, phase, but was peripheral at best to the third phase characterized by the development of chemical, steel and electrical industry. It was in the period from about 1850 to 1880 that it was in the forefront of industrial development; and from then until about 1910 – the time of Home Rule agitation – the momentum of that development carried it forward. In the textile business, the region followed the slightly unusual progression from home-produced linen to mill-produced cotton to mill-produced linen. The area around Belfast had become the centre of the linen industry by the late eighteenth century. The cotton jenny was introduced to Belfast in 1780, and a manufacture developed in water-powered spinning mills. In 1790 one of Watt's steam engines was installed in Lisburn. But by the middle of the century the technology had been developed that made the large-scale production of linen possible, and power-looms took over from about 1850. In 1851 the lease of part of the Queen's Island on the Lagan to Thompson and Kirwan founded the great shipbuilding industry that eventually was to be known under the name Harland and Wolff.

But by the end of the Great War those days were over. What had been the heartland of the most advanced industry and technology in the world – that northerly region of the British Isles that included Merseyside, Tyneside and Clydeside, Birmingham and Belfast – had entered its long period of decline. New industrial and technological revolutions had happened elsewhere. Throughout the 1920s and the 1930s, east Ulster was economically depressed compared with other parts of the world, and since the world as a whole was deeply depressed in the 1930s the region around Belfast suffered even more severely.

Organizers and agitators endeavouring to rouse the industrial workers of east Ulster to a sense of class solidarity at the turn of the century encountered not only the usual difficulty of persuading skilled workers to join their cause to that of unskilled workers, and male workers to make common cause with female workers, but the added difficulty of trying to persuade Protestant and Catholic workers that their class should unite them. That was not how the workers in general saw it. There were, of course, exceptions, and in the highly class-conscious time just before the Great War, the organizers of interdenominational labour had a few ephemeral successes. Among others, both Jim Larkin and James Connolly* took part in these efforts before moving south. But by the time of the great Dublin lockout of 1913, when labour unsucccessfully confronted capital in a long struggle and a small section of the Irish working class committed itself to revolutionary activity, in the North, Protestant labour confronted Catholic labour on the question of Home Rule and the Union. Thereafter, North and

*James Larkin (1876–1947): Irish Labour leader, founder of first major unskilled workers' trade union in Ireland; James Connolly (1868–1916): Irish socialist organizer and theorist of republican socialism, executed for his leading role in the rising of 1916.

South, the national question supplanted the class struggle.

From time to time in the North, socialist and labour candidates won small successes in elections, but it was never possible to maintain these or to expand them. It was only necessary for the Unionist government to indicate, persuasively, that a split loyalist vote would endanger the Union, to bring the workers back to their primary allegiance.

Among the workers, recurrent periods of street violence had led to recurrent segregation, forming persistent patterns in employment and residence. In any given area, in times of riot, those who were in a small minority – whether in the workplace or in the home –were driven out, chased back across an invisible boundary to 'their own side'. So, there were Catholic districts and Protestant districts in the cities and towns of the province. The Catholic family living peacefully perhaps for years in a Protestant street – or vice versa – always faced the danger that in time of violence neighbours who had been friendly the day before would become a mob to smash in door and windows or worse. The strict territoriality of the Protestant-Catholic divide would be reinforced. Occasionally, in times of extreme violence, the matter would go further and one side would attempt to *gain* territory from the other. This is what happened in Belfast in August 1969 when Protestant mobs followed the RUC into Catholic territory: the burning of Bombay Street was only one among the ensuing episodes. It is what happened to Protestant houses in the Lenadoon Estate. When those houses were allocated to Catholics after rebuilding, it led to a riot on 9 July 1972 that caused the breakdown of a truce between the Provisional IRA and the British.

Similarly, segregation occurred in the work place, Catholics being repeatedly, in nineteenth- and twentieth-century episodes of violence, driven out of the shipyards and engineering works. This was reinforced by a policy of discrimination in employment, employers collaborating with their employees in enforcing the segregation. The more heavily populated parts of the province were largely those with substantial Protestant majorities; so the discrimination operated chiefly against Catholics. But in some areas, where the substantial local majority was Catholic, it operated against Protestants. An effect of the segregation was that some occupations – including most in the shipbuilding and engineering industries – were associated with Protestants, others – including many in the service industries – were associated with Catholics. There were many Catholic women working in the textile mills, and this led to unusual social situations, as in Derry, where there was high unemployment among men but low-paid employment was available for women: the women went out to work; the men stayed at home and drew the dole.

Such circumstances offered little scope for socialist agitation, although quite a few optimists tried. If republicans of the right persuaded themselves that loyalists were misled from the path of true Irishness, republicans of the left indulged themselves in the delusion that the perversity of loyalist workers resulted from a clever form of capitalist exploitation: they were fooled by being offered a false privilege that divided them from their Catholic fellow-workers; and this masked the real class division between workers and bosses. It is true, of course, that the confessional division did the workers no good at all in respect of better wages or conditions. But the cause may be quite deep-rooted. The failure to develop a keen and exclusive class consciousness was something they shared with the great mass of British workers and also with the workers of the Irish Free State, virtually throughout the Depression years. The Irish workers had been beaten in the great lockout of 1913, the British in the general strike of 1926, and all were amenable to forms of manipulation – not merely religious – that did not apply in the same way to their fellows in Continental Europe.

Rural Protestant Ulster, or parts of it, retained through the inter-war years much of the deferential character that marked British society. The rural gentry were not regarded in Protestant Ulster, as they were in most of Ireland, as an alien and unwanted breed. On the contrary, they were the natural leaders of the Protestant people, derived, in the eyes of those they led, from the Plantation, like the tenants, the craftsmen and the small shop-keepers. They had developed, even more strongly than their Scottish or English counterparts, the tradition of military service: Northern Ireland was a nursery of British generals.

They owned a great deal of the land of the province and some of them had, like the British gentry and aristocracy, added to their wealth during and after the Industrial Revolution and maintained their position in political society. Officers and ex-officers of this class played a very significant part in the organization of the UVF in 1913 and 1914 and thereafter, and in the overseeing of the special constabulary after 1920. They were present again, at least on the sidelines, in 1971 and 1972, when the UDA was being organized into a province-wide force; although, as the regular British army took over the fight against the IRA from Stormont, and as a special Ulster regiment, the UDR, was formed to replace the B-Specials, the UDA soon took a separate course.

For the greater part of the half-century in which Northern Ireland had limited self government, that government was headed by members of this class. Sir James Craig, later Lord Craigavon, of a whiskey-distilling family that had become landed gentry, was Prime Minister from 1921 until the Second World War, to be succeeded briefly by J. M. Andrews, then by Sir Basil Brooke (Viscount Brookeborough), descendant of a Sir Basil Brooke who had been granted broad acres in the seventeenth-century Plantation and had rebuilt Donegal Castle. Brookeborough was Prime Minister until 1963, when he was succeeded by Captain Terence O'Neill, descended from the Chichesters – among the richest of the seventeenth-century colonists – and from the Earls of Tyrone. When O'Neill was forced from office in the crisis of 1969, he was succeeded by his cousin James Chichester-Clark.

It was evidence that a revolution of sorts had occurred or was occurring in Northern Ireland when Chichester-Clark in turn had to make way, in 1971, not for another landlord but for a member of an entrepreneurial-industrialist family, Brian Faulkner. The Unionist Party was still in control but it was beginning to splinter. The shift from Chichester-Clark to Faulkner was not just one of social class but was a move in the decolonization of Ulster. The landed gentry retained not only a close connection with England but a base of sorts there, sending their children to English public schools, serving in the British Army, cultivating and maintaining close personal – often marital – relations in England. Faulkner, although of military age at the time, had not joined the British armed forces even during the Second World War (conscription had not been applied in Northern Ireland throughout the War, partly because of effective Dublin policy). He replaced Chichester-Clark ostensibly because aroused unionist opinion wanted a 'hard' line in Stormont in place of a 'soft' line; but there was more to it than that. His accession signalled that, just as the Catholics of Northern Ireland had rebelled against Stormont, so now the Protestants of Northern Ireland – or a sufficient number of them – were rebelling against British efforts to manipulate or compel Stormont to accommodate the Catholics.

He tried to satisfy his constituency and demonstrate his hardness by urging on a somewhat sceptical British Tory government the implementation of internment without trial as a means of suppressing the uprising. This was worse than a mistake. The British Army had been sent in in August 1969 to prop up the Stormont government; it ended by contributing to its downfall. In 1970, the British Labour government – at that stage beginning to think in terms of a united Ireland within ten or twenty years – was defeated in a general election and replaced by Edward Heath's Tory government. The Home Secretary, then responsible for Northern Irish affairs, was the dilatory and rather shady Reginald Maudling whose attitude to his Ulster responsibility was one of bored contempt. The military commander on the ground was General Freeland who, with a Tory government at his back in the summer of that year, attempted to handle the disorder in the province with a heavy hand. He placed the whole Falls area of Belfast under curfew for several days, and sent in his soldiers to kick in the doors and bayonet the mattresses in a house-to-house search for arms, in the course of which several people were killed. The nationalists of the province, already in a state of euphoric excitement after the events of the previous two years, were provided with a readily identifiable and ancient enemy – 'Cromwell's men are here again', as the refrain of a slightly later ballad put it.

The IRA, in both its branches, began recruiting and rearming as fast as it could. In February 1971 the first British soldier was shot dead in Belfast and in March three Scottish soldiers were lured to their death in Ligoniel, as political agitation was succeeded by lethal violence in the development that led to the replacement of Chichester-Clark by Faulkner. When Faulkner's government recommended to the British a policy of internment, it was following the precedent of successful actions at times in the past when the republicans were few in number and well known to the police. 'Round up the usual suspects' was a plausible precept usually leading to success. But now the government was faced with an unprecedented popular uprising in more and more of the nationalist areas of Northern Ireland, and the British Army was adding fuel to the flames by concentrating its attention on nationalist areas.

Tim Pat Coogan illustrates the process vividly in his book, *Disillusioned Decades: Ireland 1966–87.*

Ironically, in view of the reputation it would acquire, Crossmaglen was totally uninterested in IRA activities when the troubles began. The most burning wish evinced at that stage was to be allowed to get on with their smuggling activities to and fro across the adjacent border with County Louth in the Republic. Then the British Army came and its attentions grew more burdensome as troubles mounted elsewhere in the province . . . What happened was that one fine day outside the Springfield Road Barracks a car backfired and a soldier panicked and accidentally shot dead an innocent motorist, a man from Crossmaglen. Hostility grew towards the troops, who retaliated with increased house searches. Weapons were often planted in the process (so that intelligence might be extracted in the resultant interrogations of the occupants). Standard operating procedure included stopping and beating up young men thought to be likely IRA material. They were, but not the way the Army thought of them. As a member of the Irish Special Branch observed to me, 'The Army created the IRA'.

(I can add that I have myself observed the RUC 'creating the IRA' in a very similar way in the city of Armagh, almost fifteen years later.)

So, when in August 1971, mass arrests were made with the intention of interning the active IRA members and so suppressing the uprising, it was a blind operation. The formula of 'the usual suspects' no longer applied. RUC intelligence was out of date in a situation which had changed dramatically within two years; while the British Army hadn't yet built up its own intelligence. Hundreds of arrests were made, mostly of the wrong people. The two IRAs expanded even more rapidly and violence became widespread and severe throughout the province.

There was much talk, then and later, of the danger of a 'Protestant backlash', but in fact, in the 1960s as in 1912, the 'Protestant backlash' had come first – essentially responding not directly to Catholic or nationalist action but to the effects of British parliamentary action. The first serious street violence for many years had occurred in the 'tricolour riots' during the British general election of 1964, when loyalists attacked republican election offices in Belfast that were flying the Irish national flag. The first murders in what was to be a long and dreary series were the late-night murders of two young Catholic men in the summer of 1966, by members of the newly formed UVF. The UVF (which simply stole the name of the province-wide organization formed in 1913 to resist Home Rule) had announced in the name of the Adjutant of its 1st Belfast Battalion that it was declaring war on the IRA (then quiescent) and that it would execute 'mercilessly and without hesitation' known IRA men. The early bombs – exploding in reservoirs serving Belfast – that helped to bring down Captain O'Neill were (as was later established) loyalist bombs. The first RUC man to be killed in these troubles met his death in a loyalist riot in Belfast in late 1969.

But by 1970 and 1971 the rapidly spreading violence chiefly involved nationalists and the security forces, and it reached a scale after the fiasco of internment that caused the British government to decide to undo the settlement of more than half a century earlier and to begin again to try to answer the 'Irish Question'. Northern Ireland lost its parliament and its home rule government in 1972. The Irish question became more clearly what it had in truth always been: the Anglo-Irish question.

9

The British Dimension

The United States of America has not many, but several things in common with Ireland, one of which is that both countries have been under British government. For the Americans this experience ended more than two hundred years ago; for the greater part of Ireland, it ended less than seventy years ago.

There are of course differences in the way in which British rule, in its day, operated and in how it came into being in the two countries. But the differences are not as great as might have been expected. In both cases an extended process of migration and colonization lay in the background. Movements for independence were conducted at least partly by people who were aiming to separate from a system that they regarded as being to some extent their own inheritance. Independence was a divorce that did not altogether deny a shared, or family, history.

The main difference lies in the attitudes taken to the 'indigenous inhabitants'. The British in the late-eighteenth-century quarrel with the American colonials took up the cause of the Amerindians whose land the colonials (with earlier British backing) had been stealing and wished to continue to steal. British interference with the process of annexation is one of the grievances listed in the Declaration of Independence, although it is less frequently quoted than some other passages in that famous document.

But in Ireland the distinction between settlers and natives was in the first place more blurred. Those regarded as indigenous or aboriginal (insofar as intermarriage allowed this distinction to be continued) were white Europeans who, by the late eighteenth century, were English-speaking in larger and larger numbers and were adopting more and more of the manners and customs of Great Britain. By the early twentieth century, when independence was

116

finally achieved, this process of acculturation was very far advanced. But so, on the part of the separatists, was a process of notional rejection of the English culture generally adopted, and of notional revival of the largely lost indigenous culture.

Obviously any comparison of something that happened more than two hundred years ago with something that happened less than seventy years ago must take into account the enormous changes that have occurred in the world in the interval. When America became independent, for example, its population size was comparable to that of Ireland (although its geographical size, in the thirteen colonies, was vastly greater than Ireland's). Ireland's population today is only about 25 per cent greater than it was in 1780. America's population is more than fifty times greater.

Still, it is possible to make comparisons. The old British connection continues to manifest itself in many and various ways in America, after two hundred years. There is no doubt that Americans, of all opinions and prejudices, look on the British as being different from most other foreigners (the Irish, incidentally, also enjoy to a great extent a similarly 'not-quite-foreign' status). There are Anglophiles and Anglophobes, but there is still, overall, a special relationship. Americans, when it comes down to it, regard Britain as being responsible for much of what they value in their own heritage (especially in politics).

Here the dissimilarity with independent Ireland is striking. Irish independence came about at a time when, for obvious reasons – in the middle of a struggle to separate from the United Kingdom – what was emphasized in the Irish heritage was what distinguished Ireland from Great Britain, and in particular from England. Great emphasis was placed on the Gaelic tradition. Irish was the national language and was widely referred to by people whose native language was English as 'our native language'. Those elements in Irish history that appeared to be rooted in indigenous culture were valued above elements that were plainly imported or introduced under English dominion or influence. The impetus of the effort to maintain this distinction carried on well after the achievement of independence, but from the beginning there were indications that the effort was not wholehearted.

The cultural effort in question was in large part an attempt to revive Irish. People who were not in sympathy with it used to make a slightly fatuous objection to the Irish language. The language wasn't 'modern'; it lacked vocabulary for business, science, technology in the present-day world. Now, any living language can cope with the modern world. Languages and vocabulary change all the time anyway. There was a deeper contradiction concerning the use of Irish in the early years of the Irish State.

The larger problem arises from the use of the language simply as an assertion of difference rather than for the sake of what it was and what it embodied. It is not that the indigenous language of the country lacked a technical vocabulary; it is that the Irish spoken and written by the revivalists lacked indigenous values. The language was used too much to 'translate' artificially; to express ideas that belonged to the culture of English and could therefore be better expressed in English. There was no point in having *Comic Cuts* in Irish in an English-speaking Ireland.

This gave rise to a kind of weariness, found in formulas that evaded the real problems of cultural change. It was Éamon de Valera's custom to open his public speeches with a few words in Irish – 'Focal tosaigh dos na Gaeilgeoirí', as he often introduced them – 'a word first for those who like to speak Irish'. This epitomized the evasion. Tokenism prevailed. Even in the first Dáil in 1919, the elected assembly which declared the Republic that had been proclaimed in 1916, English was used, after token homage had been paid to the national language. And when it came to serious business, like the Treaty debates, almost all of substance that was said was said in English. Compulsory Irish never existed in independent Ireland. All that was compulsory was that the language should be taught in the schools. That it was often taught very badly was another matter.

So the British heritage was both denied and accepted at the same time, but in a much more confusing and obscuring way than had happened in America. The Americans accepted the British cultural and political tradition as it had come to them, but rejected aspects of British culture (such as the formal social hierarchy) that had developed poorly if at all in the colonies. The Irish State was founded by people who accepted, much more readily and unthinkingly than the American Founding Fathers, a great deal of the

British political inheritance, but attempted to reject selected elements of British culture (without realizing how much of it, in fact, they were tacitly accepting).

The result is what is perhaps the deepest of the many ambiguities in the political life of the Republic, a mismatching structural fault that goes right down through the crust of its political philosophy. The State had discovered no adequate way of adjusting to the still powerful neighbour who was once the metropolitan power. This failure has been made clear since the 'Thirty Years War' of the North began; but the breakdown of civilization in Ulster has worked wonderfully to concentrate at least some minds south of the Border. The failure of Irish governments, before 1969, to articulate a policy in relation to the North that was both responsible and credible undoubtedly contributed to the bloody anarchy that occurred there; but the effort has since been made to undo that failure.

Passing over the Irish Free State's dealings with the United Kingdom within the framework of the Empire and Commonwealth, it is possible to say that for nearly half a century Ireland had to deal with Britain in two distinct contexts: Britain-in-Ireland and Britain-outside-Ireland. Britain-outside-Ireland provided the principal problems in external affairs for the Irish State, but they were, as it were, benign problems on the whole. With no other country had Ireland such close ties (literally a million of them on the personal level alone, of Irish people settled in Great Britain). Ireland's main markets were in Britain, as well as its principal sources of supply for many goods and commodities. British and Irish views on the world at large were often fairly similar. Irish neutrality in the Second World War was partly a reaction to the difficulties encountered in the other context – that of Britain-in-Ireland – as was the initial Irish refusal to join NATO. But Britain and Ireland entered the European Community hand in hand.

Britain-in-Ireland provides a different kind of problem. In the first place it is an old problem, whose difficulty is increased, not diminished, by propinquity and long experience. The Irish, for example, North and South, loyalist and nationalist, are acutely aware of that aspect of English governmental character summed up by Britain's nearest neighbour on the other side – France – as 'perfidious Albion'. They simply do not trust the English. What is perceived as perfidy, however, is probably better described as humbug – self-serving self-deception rather than consciously dishonest dealings with others.

It must be remembered that British governments down the years have had to adjust to the decline in British power and to accommodate to political ideas that, in the heyday of the Raj, were anathema. The majority of Irish people, virtually for as long as it has been possible to ascertain their views, have not wanted to be ruled by the English or by the surrogates of the English. But 'national self determination' was not, to past British administrations, an acceptable idea. British negotiators opposed this very concept at Versailles in 1919, for example – the idea Wilson had stated as a basis for the post-war settlement of Europe – largely because it would not suit their own imperialist interests; and in particular because it would embarrass them in Ireland. Wilson, it turned out, purveyed a fair amount of humbug himself – as Lenin had shrewdly noted – and the issue did not arise at that time as a serious difficulty for the British.

They compromised on Ireland not because they had accepted any such principle but because they could not summon up the moral and other resources needed to defeat an Irish population that fought them with determination. Circumstances alter cases, and nowadays British governments are strongly in favour of 'national self-determination'. In the British general election of 1918 – fought throughout Ireland on the issue of the Union – the overwhelming vote in Ireland for a republic was not accepted as a legitimate 'self-determination', even apart from the special question of Ulster. But to an extent, the determination of something over a fifth of the electorate, concentrated in Ulster, not to be forced into an Irish republic, was respected.

In 1982 the British did not ostensibly conduct the war in the South Atlantic because the Argentinians had seized a British possession (the legal 'ownership' of the Malvinas, or Falklands, was debatable), but in support of the self-determination of the islanders – although a determination of the islanders that they wished to be British citizens had recently been rejected. And today, Great Britain is committed (by the Hillsborough Agreement) to support the self-determination of Northern Ireland. The British, although capable of ruthlessness in war and of the callous calculation of interest, and corresponding willingness at times to override the interests of others that characterize the experience of power, are yet a civilized and humane people. The wishes and interests of the people of Northern Ireland are by no means excluded from the reasoning of their rulers. But that is not the whole story.

It is probable that the majority of the people of Great Britain would, on balance, like to see a withdrawal from Northern Ireland. The rulers, however, have responsibility, as well as their own opinions. And they tend, in some of these matters, to have different opinions from the majority of the people. The long experience and tradition of empire have left the minds of the governors coloured by what are, by now, complex and contradictory impulses. That experience, it should be remembered, has been to some extent renewed in Northern Ireland over the past two decades, notably by the establishment of proconsular rule there.

The current Northern Ireland Office is quite an oddity, constitutionally considered, but there is no doubt that it accommodates the nostalgia (focussed so much recently on British India) that is plainly felt by many people in Britain for the days when they could handle, in lofty and imperial fashion, the affairs of various lots of natives. When Queen Elizabeth II came to the throne as a young woman there was much wistful talk in Britain about a 'new Elizabethan Age'. Instead, there was the end of Empire, and every evidence was provided of economic and political decline. In the 1960s, the young people of the day seemed to shrug off the whole imperial past and find liberation for themselves thereby from all kinds of conventions and constraints; content, it would seem, that Britain should become a Sweden or a Denmark, attempting to provide a good life for all its people rather than to bestride the world. But that phase has passed, and the Britain governed now for more than a decade by Mrs Thatcher is a very different place. She herself has advocated a return to Victorian values (although the values she offers are not quite that) and clearly would like a return to Victorian 'greatness'.

The upheaval in Northern Ireland was, in some part at least, a manifestation of the spirit of the 1960s. The 'Welfare State' established in the United Kingdom after the War, among other things placed higher education within the reach of virtually the whole population, poor as well as rich, and encouraged the foundation of new universities, polytechnics and third-level schools that gave great scope to people whose views and outlook were much at variance with those of the masters and servants of the old Empire. The British Welfare State, especially through its educational provisions, effectively undid the discriminatory restraints placed by Stormont government on Catholics in Northern Ireland, and enabled a young articulate generation to take to the streets in the late 1960s demanding civil rights.

But within a few years the imperial graduates were back in control for a while, shortly to be overtaken by the neo-conservatives of the Heath and Thatcher kind – a very different breed from the older conservatives. One of the important political struggles of recent years in Britain has been within the Conservative and Unionist Party, between 'gentlemen' and 'players'; and for the moment the 'players' have won hands down. The conflict was between social rather than economic classes, although it had implications for the renewal of real class war. The symbolic moment came when the troops returned from the South Atlantic. Their victory parade was held in the City of London, where the salute was taken by Mrs Thatcher, not in Whitehall, where the salute would have been taken by the Queen.

The crude power of money was being asserted as against the more complex exercise of power by a combination of money and prescriptive tradition embodying pseudo-feudal concepts of responsibility for the weak: *noblesse oblige*. And what was involved in terms of immediate policy was to bring the British people to obedience. Not only must the power of the trades unions be broken but what remained of the spirit of the 1960s must be crushed. The levelling effect, such as it was, of the Welfare State must be undone, and a clear gulf set again between rich and poor. The Americans, pursuing, under Reagan, a similar policy in the 1980s, were coming to speak of an 'underclass'. Such a class, anything up to 15 per cent of the population, excluded from such minimum well-being as could be provided for the bulk of the people, was necessary to make the proposed system work: an awful example stimulating the fear that would help drive the new economy. And that new economy included a very large, and growing, service sector, employing

122

masses of people in low-paid dead-end jobs, people many of whom would be ready and willing to take the jobs of industrial workers who no longer, in a more and more automated world, had skills sufficiently arcane to protect them.

These developments were manifest in 1970, when the Heath government took office. For the intense personal dislike that exists between Edward Heath and Margaret Thatcher should not obscure the fact that she rides the same horse from which she unsaddled him. Heath humbled the postal workers but was beaten in 1974 by the miners, and then defeated in two rapidly successive general elections, allowing a five-year interval of Labour government. The trade-union leaders then overreached themselves in challenging the government, and the electorate turned back to the Tories, now led by Mrs Thatcher. She not only reduced the miners but demoralised the Labour Party, watched one of its battalions break and run, and then turned to reduce her own party to submission. She has been busy for ten years remaking Britain, in a drastic way that few would have thought possible in 1970. Among other things, Britain is a much more unequal, much less free, much more violent, dangerous and crime-ridden, much less pleasant, although notionally more prosperous society than it was in 1970, and its north-south division is arguably now more radical than Ireland's.

To discuss usefully Great Britain's part in the Northern Ireland conflict it is necessary to bear in mind that British politics had many other concerns in the 1970s and 1980s. The Ulster conflict is quite commonly presented as two-sided. Effective British expositions – since the embarrassment caused by the civil rights agitation of the late 1960s and the publicity they received, in the days when Bernadette Devlin was Joan of Arc – have ensured that most of the short reports that now appear occasionally around the world refer quite simplistically to a Catholic-Protestant confrontation within Northern Ireland. On the other hand, where IRA propaganda has been reasonably effective – as among some Irish-American communities and groups – the conflict is seen as one between IRA freedom fighters and British oppressors. It is of course neither of these. It is three-sided.

The aims of two of the sides – the unionists and the nationalists – are moderately clear. What do the British want? This is the question not sufficiently often asked. It is possible but unlikely that the British do not know what they want; that British governments, still, after twenty years, are cobbling up policy from day to day, year to year, not knowing where they are going in the long run. It is somewhat more likely that British policy is paralysed, because there are powerful contrary views among the policy-makers and because other concerns have priority, so that there cannot be a sufficient concentration of attention and effort on this one to resolve the contradiction.

Taking the long view back to the Union, as has been argued earlier, it would seem that the general direction of British policy has been to move out of Ireland, but that the process of withdrawal is glacially slow. And the direction of the movement is from time to time temporarily reversed. Historically, the chief British interest in Ireland has been strategic, although there have been many other interests too. At least since the sixteenth century Ireland has been a potential danger to Britain, not particularly because of an Irish threat but because the country offered a base, with a population hostile to England, for a Continental power to turn Britain's defences. The Spaniards played on English fears in this respect in the sixteenth century, as the French did later. In 1796 a large French force sailed for Ireland and was prevented only by storms from landing an army that would have been welcomed by a great insurrection. As late as the end of 1940, Hitler asked for the acquiescence of the South (which was refused) should he send to County Down the parachute troops that in fact he used half a year later to seize Crete. When the Treaty was being negotiated and debated in 1921 a major British concern was that, whatever measure of independence Ireland might achieve, there should be full and adequate safeguards against the use of the island as a base from which Britain might be attacked. Britain in fact retained several naval bases on the coast of the Irish Free State; but these were handed over in 1938. While the British convoys couldn't use them in the Second World War, Irish ports and bases were equally not available to Britain's enemies.

The technological transformation of warfare, including naval warfare, since then has reduced if not abolished Ireland's strategic importance for Britain in this respect. British and American

124

submarines that might launch nuclear missiles at the Soviet Union operate regularly in the Irish Sea (occasionally sinking fishing trawlers whose nets they foul), as no doubt do Russian submarines. (Belfast is about half way, as the missile flies, between Boston and Omsk.) But it is doubtful if the control of Northern Ireland adds significantly to Britain's advantage in this respect: there are adequate bases just a few miles away in western Scotland.

On the other hand the collaboration of the whole of Ireland in a European military alliance would have obvious, if marginal, advantages for such an alliance. The Republic of Ireland is not a member of NATO. The United Kingdom, of course, is. The European Community has no connection as such with NATO, but all its member states except Ireland are also members of the alliance. As the Community moves towards closer political union, the pressure must come on Ireland (as it already has) to make a military commitment too. This, however, has only an indirect bearing on Britain's interest in Northern Ireland.

Northern Ireland is not a source of revenue to Great Britain, although it once briefly was, in a small way. On the contrary, the balance of fiscal transfers has been heavily towards Northern Ireland for many years. The province, which had a period of industrial growth in the twenty years after the Second World War, has for years been, economically, the most depressed region of the United Kingdom and its social services are a drain on the British exchequer, as are the many subventions and subsidies provided for its infrastructure and failing industries.

The extra costs since 1969 arising from the violence in Northern Ireland (falling on both Britain and the province, but obviously chiefly on Britain) were estimated by the New Ireland Forum in the 1983 report, *The Cost of Violence arising from the Northern Ireland Crisis since 1969*, at £11,064,000, including Exchequer costs (£6,274,000) and economic costs (£4,790,000) (in 1982 pounds).

Obviously, then, Great Britain holds Northern Ireland at a considerable, although not insupportable, monetary cost. There is also a cost to Britain in soldiers' lives and injuries. But it must be remembered that the British are a bellicose people, whose army has been in action somewhere in the world in every year since the end of the Second World War (and indeed in most years of the past 250). It has been argued that Northern Ireland is an ideal training ground for the army, with a casualty rate sufficiently low to be tolerable and sufficiently high to keep the soldiers keen and alert, while the restraints imposed upon them by functioning among civilians teach them discipline.

There are other costs, some less obvious. From time to time the violence of Northern Ireland spills over into Britain, as it also does into the Republic, and numbers of people have been killed by bombs in Great Britain. They included Airey Neave, Conservative spokesman on Northern Ireland, who was killed by an INLA bomb in the car park of the House of Commons in 1979, just before his party defeated Labour in general election and Mrs Thatcher became Prime Minister, and people killed when a bomb exploded in Brighton in 1984, partly demolishing the hotel that housed Mrs Thatcher and most of her government while they attended the Conservative Party conference. And a member of the British royal family, Lord Mountbatten, was killed in 1979 in the waters of the Republic when a Provisional IRA bomb exploded in his boat. In 1976 the British Ambassador to Ireland was assassinated in Dublin – by means of a mine.

The less obvious costs include the damage that is done to a once open and liberal society, such as that of post-war Britain, by the ever increasing emphasis on security, the fear of terrorism, and the development by the State of more and more effective methods of control of unruly populations. Policing in Britain, for example, has changed over the twenty-year period from the older English style of maintaining the law and the peace through cooperation with the public, by unarmed, friendly and often solitary bobbies on the beat, towards the colonial style that emphasizes order rather than law and that usually requires paramilitary organization. The British police forces, in other words, have become somewhat more like the RUC or the Hong Kong Police than they used to be.

It might seem then, that Britain has no good reason for staying in any part of Ireland. But there are several. In the first place, the greater part (probably about 75 per cent at the moment) of the people of Northern Ireland wishes Britain to remain in Ireland, at least for the present, and a smaller majority of the people wishes that presence to be permanent. And the British government has made commitments to respect that wish. It is not to be expected that a state will readily force out from under its jurisdiction people who wish to remain there. But it does happen from time to time in the process of imperial disengagement. Northern Ireland, however, is not a colony like Hong Kong. It is a part of the United Kingdom, even if a part that is given special, separate and unusual treatment, to the extent that since 1985, by treaty right, the Irish government sits in on the management of its affairs.

There is also the intangible, but real, matter of prestige. It was interesting, in London in 1982, when the war was being fought in the South Atlantic, to talk to English people who had for years held 'left-wing', anti-imperialist and anti-militarist views. Shame-facedly, against their own reasoning and judgment, quite a few of them admitted that they had a sneaking feeling of pride on discovering that the old lion not only could still roar, but had teeth. How much more then, did people of 'right-wing' views support not only the ferocious war against Argentina, but every act and gesture indicating that Britain was still a power in the world.

Withdrawal finally from Ireland would contribute a deadening finality to the end of Empire. Yet the Empire has ended; and many other changes have taken place and are taking place in the world. Northern Ireland has become more than an embarrassment to the British. It is an incalculable, seemingly insoluble, problem, and therefore a continuing nuisance and a potential danger.

These contradictions may help to explain the previous veerings and the current paralysis of British policy since the troubles began twenty years ago. At the beginning of the upheaval there seemed to be, broadly, two alternatives: a continuation of the home rule, Stormont, arrangement; or a united Ireland governed from Dublin. Other possibilities, such as a renewed Anglo-Irish link in a federation of the British Isles, were not technically or politically feasible. Some British politicians clearly thought that, in the long run, it would be a united Ireland, and that the British government, in so far as it was concerned with long-term plans, should bear this in mind. Harold Wilson, when he was out of office in 1971, aired the notion of aiming at a united Ireland within fifteen years. The negotiations conducted on behalf of the British Tory government with the IRA in 1972 and on behalf of the Labour government in

1974–75, led people on all sides at least to suspect that the British were considering withdrawal. And there are many indications that this option has been kept open: in both long-term economic planning and long-term political planning in Britain, a distancing from Northern Ireland is evident. The final withdrawal of governmental subvention from the Belfast shipyard, for example, announced in 1989, is in line with the restructuring of the British shipbuilding industry of a decade earlier.

But in the mid-1970s, when there were many such indications, there were political developments in Britain itself which would have made talk of withdrawal from Ireland inopportune. Nationalist parties in both Wales and Scotland were advocating home rule. This would involve a drastic constitutional change in Britain, and the Queen indicated a displeasure at the prospect which was shared by many, conservatives in particular. When the case was put to them the Welsh voters elected unambiguously to preserve the Union as it was. The Scots, by a narrow plurality, voted for home rule, but did not provide the two-thirds majority required to put it into effect.

The government of Harold Wilson had been taken off guard by the Ulster civil rights agitation that began in 1968 – as had the Stormont and Dublin governments. Stormont's clumsy attempts, backed by loyalist violence, to suppress the agitation drew to Northern Ireland world attention that was unwelcome to the British. The initial reaction of the Westminster politicians was to call to task their subordinates in Stormont whom they blamed not just for inept handling of the current agitation but for their misgovernment over many years. The early judicial inquiries into the Ulster troubles found against Stormont, and the British put severe pressure on the Unionists to carry out reforms in the province. This led immediately to the end of one-party unionism; since the government politicians in Stormont, responsible to Westminster, who were obliged to carry out the reforms, at once lost the support of large numbers of loyalists. The British now were faced not just with the civil rights agitation in Northern Ireland but with a loyalist revolt against a Stormont government that was making belated and grudging concessions (at the behest of Westminster) to the civil rights demands. And the Catholic nationalists stepped up their demands and increased their agitation as they saw the opportunity, after half a century, of ending the Unionist rule under which they had chafed. When the Labour government put the army on the streets in August 1969 to relieve Stormont, it threw fuel on the fire. And the Heath government that succeeded Labour in 1970 compounded the error.

The formation of the Provisional IRA, the beginning of their bombing campaign, the attacks on the British Army, the confused effects of internment: none of these sufficiently mitigated or clarified the problem. Very large numbers of people were marching in the streets, proclaiming to the world that they were deprived of their civil rights. In his manual, *Low-Intensity Operations*, General Kitson, a counter-insurgency expert who advised the British army at the beginning of its operations in Ulster, wrote of movements like that demanding civil rights in Northern Ireland:

There are two main difficulties which confront the organisers of a non-violent campaign when it comes to controlling their followers, both of which are capable of being exploited by the Government. The first of these is that a large number of people have to be involved compared, for example, to the numbers required to conduct a programme of sabotage or terrorism, and the second is that the participants themselves are not disciplined members of a clandestine organisation, but crowds of citizens or groups of students who may resent tight, political organisation as part of their beliefs . . . With the major weaknesses of non-violent action in mind, it is possible to consider a general framework of operations suitable for combating it. For the purposes of this study no account will be taken of the simplest method of all, which is to suppress the movement by the ruthless application of naked force, because although non-violent campaigns are particularly vulnerable to this sort of action, it is most unlikely that the British government, or indeed any Western government would be politically able to operate on these lines even if it wanted to do so.

Reluctantly accepting this limitation, the writer goes on to say that:

In practical terms the most promising line of approach lies in separating the mass of those engaged in the campaign from the leadership by the judicious promise of concessions, at the same time imposing a period of calm by the use of government forces backed up by statements to the effect that most of the concessions can only be implemented once the life of the country returns to normal.

However, although it is this second 'practical' line of approach that was on the whole followed in Northern Ireland (where the British government, like the American in Vietnam for a long time, appears sometimes to have derived political decisions from military advice), the simplest method, the application of 'naked force', was attempted with remarkable success at the beginning of 1972. On Sunday, 30 January, soldiers opened fire on a large civil rights demonstration which, like all such assemblies (especially in Derry) at that time, included an unruly stone-throwing element. This was not another Amritsar massacre, a flash of imperial rage against the scandal of insubordinate natives. It was much more restrained and calculated: aimed fire, singling out youths and young men, of whom thirteen were killed; a nicely measured whiff of grapeshot.

The effective non-violent civil rights movement came to a sudden end, such movements being indeed, as General Kitson had written, 'particularly vulnerable to this sort of action'. The adverse political effects were soon dissipated by the burning of the British embassy in Dublin on the following Wednesday, by the loss of nerve of the Northern civil rights movement when it came to organizing a great non-violent demonstration at Newry the following Saturday, in which masses of people from the Republic were initially intended to join, by the Official IRA's inept atrocity in reprisal at Aldershot, and by the Provisional IRA's massacre of citizens later, in Belfast (on 'Bloody Friday'), in Claudy, and elsewhere.

The rapid setting-up of a tribunal of inquiry into the Derry shooting also went a long way towards undoing adverse political effects, in spite of the fact that the inquiry was conducted by Lord Chief Justice Widgery with such blatant bias as to bring British justice in Ireland into contempt, not for the first or the last time.

The success of 'Bloody Sunday' was in ending the effective civil rights movement, and preparing the way to present the political conflict in Northern Ireland as a struggle of law against terrorism. It is true that the conflict now degenerated into a very unpleasant condition of sporadic violence. But at the time it wasn't foreseen that this would continue for long. To quote again from General Kitson's book (published in 1971), he wrote on his opening page that: 'It can be argued that the recent past has been exceptional, that Northern Ireland and Vietnam will both be settled within five years and that with the withdrawal of all but a small remnant of the British Army into Europe, the requirement to fight insurgents or to take part in peace-keeping operations will cease . . .'

General Kitson was more or less right about Vietnam. About Ireland he displays the common British failure – too close to the subject, too uninterested, too involved – to understand. The American J. Bowyer Bell, a year earlier wrote in his book *The Secret Army* that '. . . what is peculiar to the IRA, by contrast with most revolutionary groups, is persistence in the face of failure'.

The assertion of imperial authority in the shots of the 30th of January was logically and swiftly followed by the resumption by the imperial government of direct rule over Northern Ireland. This, coming shortly after the reforms that Stormont had been forced to make, gave rise to the constitutional anomaly described adequately in the words of the Ulster Unionist Party's discussion paper of 1984, *The Way Forward*:

In only one part of the United Kingdom, namely, Northern Ireland, are major services subject to no real democratic control. In Northern Ireland alone do employees and professional staff who would normally take their instructions directly from elected representatives, take their orders from the civil servants of the Government Departments at Stormont. There are in Northern Ireland, no indigenous representatives who decide and direct policy on major services and who themselves are answerable to their electorates for their stewardship. The Stormont civil servants are answerable to no-one but the Secretary of State for Northern Ireland and his team of ministers all of whom are on short term commissions . . . This complete absence of local democracy came about not by design but by chance. The Review

Body on Local Government in Northern Ireland under the chairmanship of Sir Patrick Macrory submitted its report in 1970. The Macrory Report, as it came to be known, provided for the abolition of the County and County Borough Councils and recommended that their functions and powers should be transferred to the appropriate Stormont ministries so that Stormont would have fulfilled the dual function of a Parliament in the ordinary sense and as a Metropolitan or Regional Authority in the Local Government sense . . . The abolition of Stormont by Mr Heath could not have come at a worst time as, by then, the structure of County and County Borough Councils was being dismantled. There was, therefore, no elected body or bodies to run major services that passed by default into the hands of civil servants and the nominated Area Boards . . . The decision of Mr Heath's government to abolish Stormont also effectively destroyed local democratic institutions at the same time.

The suggestion that what happened 'came about by chance' is at once naive and disingenuous. Westminster was deliberately taking power from Stormont, including power that had been operated at local level only nominally through democratic institutions. All democracy had been perverted in Northern Ireland, through the peculiar nature of the province, with its 'Government without Consensus' (to quote the title of Richard Rose's excellent book, published just before the 'Troubles' began).

The Downing Street Declaration of 1969 had indicated, for the first time since the passing of the Government of Ireland Act 1920, that the British government was willing to honour its self-assumed responsibility for Northern Ireland by taking into account the rights and interests of the Catholic and nationalist minority within the six counties. However, this was at the stage when the main issue was civil rights. Once the IRA in its two forms began fighting for something quite different: separation from Britain and union with the twenty-six counties, British policy became confused. 'An acceptable level of violence' (in Maudling's words of late 1971) was one aim enunciated, and in due course, after several years, achieved. The suppression of non-violent street agitation –

132

extremely damaging to Britain's image in the world – was accomplished in 1972.

Direct rule was intended to solve the problem; but Dublin had to be both bullied and pacified in whatever other ways were available. Dublin and London were drawn together by 1972, Dublin hoping to persuade London to coerce the unionists and offer, after whatever necessary interval, a united Ireland; London hoping to disarm nationalist opinion in the South and persuade Dublin to cooperate in the pacification of both nationalists and unionists in Northern Ireland.

After 1972, against a background of continued violence in the North, the South took over, partly as the 'second guarantor' for the Northern nationalists, in the words used by Jack Lynch in his speech of August 1969, partly as a negotiator for an ultimate united Ireland, partly as the second sovereign government involved in a concern for a return to peace and order on the island of Ireland.

10

After the Union

The Union might have worked. It was, in a way, a logical development of the process by which the centre of power and wealth around London had extended its dominance over the whole island of Britain to build a major nation-state. The Union of 1707, of England and Scotland, provided a precedent of a kind. There were, however, significant differences. Scotland, throughout the Middle Ages a separate and independent kingdom, came into union with England by a steady and (after the battle of Flodden) mainly peaceful process of diplomacy and dynastic politics. When its King James VI became King of England in succession to Elizabeth in 1603, the two crowns were one. The legislative union of 1707, although there was some opposition to it, was followed by a period in which Scotsmen made a considerable impact on English, European and American thought. The parliament which, in that year, was submerged in that of Westminster had not the same consequence for its own kingdom as had the English parliament then or the Irish parliament at the end of the eighteenth century. Scotland retained a distinct legal system, and the Presbyterian remained its established church, while its native aristocracy and gentry continued for the most part on their estates. Antiquarianism fostered the word 'Britain' (from the Britannia of ancient times, and the romanticized 'Ancient Britons' who had once inhabited the whole island) as the description of the newly united kingdom, and the Scots were happy to think of themselves as 'North Britons'.

Ireland, brought under English control only after a long and difficult reconquest, and afterwards a rallying ground for defeated English causes, was of necessity treated differently. The Dublin parliament achieved legislative independence in 1782; but as that parliament was unreformed, the exercise of royal patronage and corruption enabled the English executive to manipulate or control it in most matters – even, as it turned out, with a little extra effort, in the matter of ending its own existence.

The Union was effected on 1 January 1801, at a time of European upheaval. The French Revolution had spread excitement and alarm, and the English were at war not merely with a rival nation but with radical ideas and new and powerful social and political forces. In Ireland, democratic ideas had already worked on traditional discontents and on the ambitions and imaginations of some to produce the widespread uprisings of 1798. The country was one where the universal danger of the time was particularly to be apprehended, and Pitt's government attempted to combine conciliation with firmness in securing its own rear for the confrontation with the Continental enemy. A Relief Act had already removed many disabilities from Catholics. Full emancipation was Pitt's aim; but the scheme went awry and he was unable to deliver it along with the Union – a failure ultimately fatal to the whole endeavour.

Yet many reasonable, and reasonably detached, observers thought that the Act would open the way to a solution of the Irish problem – which was seen as largely an internal one. One important provision, however, departed from the precedent of 1707. The established (Anglican/Catholic) churches of England and Ireland were to be united in one church by law established: no provision was made for the Roman Catholic complexion of most of the Irish population.

War with France continued with little intermission until 1815, and its effects helped to mask another flaw in the Union, the rapidly growing economic discrepancy between most of Britain and most of Ireland. There was a war boom, which was followed by a severe post-war slump; and it is in the period after the final defeat of Napoleon that we can discern a dangerous worsening of conditions in Ireland. Parts of Britain had already experienced the first waves of social and economic change resulting from the Industrial Revolution. The north of England, the south of Scotland and, with a little delay, part of the north-east of Ireland, were the areas where those changes first began to affect landscapes and people on a large scale. They contrasted with parts of Ireland where agricultural decline combined with rapidly growing numbers of people to produce a rural povery and destitution remarked on by all observers as something startling. One effect of the sharp contrast was that, whatever the constitutional theory, the Union did not become socially or psychologically real. And Ireland continued to be governed, thought of and treated as a separate entity.

The Union can be seen as the over-extension of a nation-state that was undergoing a remarkable transformation into an industrial giant and at the same time a world-wide trading empire. It was an expedient at a time of grave crisis, one that couldn't possibly anticipate the changes that were to come upon the world within a few decades. But in spite of the fact that agitation against the Union began so soon, and that in course of time the Union was to be largely demolished, the expedient was by no means completely unsuccessful. Under it an important and populous part of Ireland grew into a close relationship with industrialized Britain, economically, culturally, and to some extent politically, while the rest of Ireland too formed close relationships with Britain – more limited, but still enduring. The assertion of a separate identity in the recent past has not precluded most of the Irish – not merely the people of Ulster – from establishing, through migration and cultural assimilation, an insider's understanding of Britain. The Union, in other words, was partly made a reality and therefore it was partly successful.

But only partly. It had already begun to fall apart more than a century ago, not so much because adequate links had not been forged between Ireland and Britain, but because of inadequacy in the internal arrangements for Ireland. Ireland produced the elements of a new internal constitution for itself even before the parting with Britain began, through the overthrow of the order established since the end of the seventeenth century. That new internal constitution, however, is still being worked out.

The building of an Irish State has been a long-drawn-out, difficult, and at times bloody business. Lord Salisbury adverted to one of the difficulties in 1889 when he spoke of the English resistance to the granting of Irish Home Rule: 'Nations do not change their political nature like that, except through blood. It would require a subordination of all ordinary motives, a renunciation of traditions and prepossessions, a far-reaching and disciplined resolve, which is never engendered by mere persuasion, but only comes after conflict and under the pressure of military force.'

And when the third Home Rule Bill was finally passed, in 1914, it was against the background not only of the Great War, just then begun, but also of the beginning of Ireland's twentieth-century violence, violence which was already making Gladstonian Home Rule obsolete. In his book, *Englishmen and Irish Troubles*, D. G. Boyce wrote: '... After 1916 the question was not whether England would concede or withhold home rule, but the kind of relationship that a self-governing Ireland would hold with the rest of the United Kingdom, and when next the Irish question was taken up, home rule was the starting-point and not the goal.'

We have reached a similar point now. The Union, in its old sense, is undone. The present constitution of Northern Ireland is a temporary makeshift, and the rapid changes occurring in the wider world require that something more permanent replace it.

The crisis point in the present troubles was reached in the period 1971–74, when, as in 1916, things happened that have changed the whole political framework. In a few months between August 1971 and January 1972, the British Army overreached itself in Northern Ireland, causing political problems that led to a change in all the political rules. The army tortured some of the prisoners taken in the round-up of August 1971, when internment without trial was begun, using experimental techniques of sleep deprivation, hooding and exposure to high-pitched noise, and forcing men to maintain agonizingly stressful postures for long periods, as well as cruder methods such as threatening to drop blindfolded prisoners from helicopters. This was to be a source of embarrassment to the British government, which was brought by the Irish government before the European Court of Human Rights (the finding, in 1978, was that the interrogation methods amounted not to torture but to 'inhuman and degrading treatment'). The Prime Minister, Edward Heath, foreswore such methods in March 1972. The shootings of 'Bloody Sunday' in Derry, which were quite successful in one way, also caused embarrassment, but seem to have provided the occasion for the British government to make the decision to abolish Stormont and take over direct rule of the province.

The Northern Ireland Act 1972 reads, in full:

An Act to declare the law as to the legislative powers of the Parliament of Northern Ireland under section 4(1) of the Government of Ireland Act 1920, so far as relates to Her Majesty's forces and in particular to the conferment of powers, authorities, privileges or immunities on them. [24th February 1972]

Be it enacted by the Queen's most Excellent majesty, by and with the advice and consent of the Lords Spiritual and Temporal, and Commons, in this present Parliament assembled, and by the authority of the same, as follows:

1. The limitations imposed by paragraph (3) of section 4(1) of the Government of Ireland Act 1920 on the powers of the Parliament of Northern Ireland to make laws shall not have effect, and shall be deemed never to have had effect, to preclude the inclusion in laws made by that Parliament for the peace, order or good government of Northern Ireland of all provision relating to members of Her Majesty's forces as such or to things done by them when on duty, and in particular shall not preclude, and shall be deemed never to have precluded, the conferment on them by, under, or in pursuance of any such law of powers, authorities, privileges or immunities in relation to the preservation of the peace or maintenance of order in Northern Ireland. This Act may be cited as the Northern Ireland Act 1972.

In other words, retrospective immunity was conferred on the army for acts done in contravention of the Government of Ireland Act 1920 – another embarrassment, if a minor one: an instance of the process summed up in Derry and West Belfast in the words: 'Britannia waives the rules'. However, the government decided that law-and-order powers should not be in the hands of Stormont, and when the Faulkner government refused to accept this, the British government simply did away with the parliament and government of Northern Ireland and assumed direct rule of the province, in March 1972. This was the drastic change that opened up numerous possibilities. The abolition of Stormont ended a fifty-year experiment that had failed.

At this point the Official IRA declared a cease-fire, and the British government made a truce and entered into negotiations with the Provisional IRA, which soon broke down. The loyalist UVF was active, and loyalist street committees, vigilante groups and local 'defence associations' had organized themselves into the 'Ulster Defence Association', a paramilitary army of about 20,000 with units all over Northern Ireland.

In 1969, 15 people died as a result of the political violence, in 1970, 25, in 1971, 173, and in 1972, 474. This was the year in which the loss of life was greatest. At the beginning of 1973, both the United Kingdom (including, of course, Northern Ireland) and the Republic of Ireland joined the European Economic Community. By then the two governments had begun a process that was to put the Ulster problem in a different perspective.

On 30 October 1972 the British government published a Green Paper (a paper for discussion) on Northern Ireland, suggesting the formation of a Northern Ireland assembly 'capable of involving all its members constructively in ways which satisfy them and those they represent that the whole community has a part to play in the government of the Province'. It also stated that: 'In accordance with the specific pledges given by successive United Kingdom Governments, Northern Ireland must and will remain part of the United Kingdom for as long as that is the wish of the majority of the people; but that status does not preclude the necessary taking into account of what has been described in this Paper as the "Irish Dimension".'

A White Paper (policy document) of March 1973 then set out *Northern Ireland Constitutional Proposals* which showed that the government had decided to hold elections for an Assembly, 'of about 80 members', with an Executive, made up of members of the Assembly functioning as Heads of Departments of Northern Ireland. The paper stated 'the view of the Government that the Executive itself can no longer be solely based upon any single party, if that party draws its support and its elected representation virtually entirely from only one section of a divided community.'

The 'Irish dimension', further elaborated in the White Paper, led to negotiations at the end of the year, at Sunningdale in England, in which the Irish government was represented, as well as the main political parties in Northern Ireland. Mr Paisley's DUP, although invited, did not send representatives. After the 'Sunningdale Agreement' of late 1973, Northern Ireland for a few months again had a very limited home rule, with a 'power-sharing' executive, in which Unionists had a majority of places, and the main nationalist party, the SDLP, a minority. Faulkner was head of the Executive, Gerry Fitt, leader of the SDLP, his deputy. Power-sharing went against the whole precedent and practice of unionism since 1920; it was a great abnormality in terms of the procedures of Western parliamentary governments; but the combined pressures of the dangerous violence in Northern Ireland and the decision of the British government forced it on the Unionists. This, however, was an internal Northern Ireland matter, and it was tolerated.

The British White Paper and the Sunningdale Agreement had also provided for an acknowledgment of the 'Irish Dimension', through the setting up of a Council of Ireland (an idea resurrected from the Government of Ireland Act 1920 and the Treaty of 1921) to deal with matters of common interest in the island as a whole. The time came, in the early summer of 1974, to begin to implement this, and there were already politicians in the Republic speaking of it as the first step towards reunification of Ireland.

The 'Protestant backlash' now came, in the form of a general strike in Northern Ireland, organized by a number of groups who formed an *ad hoc* Ulster Workers Council, and enforced by the loyalist paramilitaries, notably the UDA, who set up checkpoints and barricades throughout the province. A Labour government, under Harold Wilson, was in office, and it hesitated, when the strike began, to take action to maintain essential services and supplies. The government condemned the strike as 'political' (which of course it avowedly was) but tried to treat it as if it were a misguided 'industrial action', sending over Len Murray of the TUC to make a fool of himself trying to lead the Ulster strikers back to work.

The Workers Association (a front for the Stalinist British and Irish Communist Organization, a rival of the anti-partitionist Communist Party of Ireland), in its *Strike Bulletin No. 1*, issued during the strike, stated that:

> This crisis could easily have been averted. David Bleakley, the only Northern Ireland Labour Party member in the Assembly, made a proposal that would have averted it. But the Executive

140

insisted on pressing ahead with its confrontation with the Loyalists . . .

Bleakley proposed a motion welcoming 'the success of power sharing', but taking note of 'the difficulties that have arisen over the meaning of the Sunningdale Agreement, particularly the ruling in the Dublin High Court that it is not possible under the present Constitution to give full recognition to Northern Ireland', and proposing that until such time as the Dublin Government is able to drop its claim to sovereignty over the North the Sunningdale Agreement should not be signed.

That was a reasonable, democratic, and statesmanlike proposal. It separated the question of power sharing from the question of a Council of Ireland, which it was urgently necessary to do. Power-sharing has been shown to work. The Council of Ireland is not necessary to power-sharing and is in fact the main danger to power-sharing. If the Council were shelved, support for power-sharing would increase rapidly in the Protestant community. And the Northern Catholic community is not particularly concerned about the Council. Catholics who cease to support the Republicans see power-sharing as the real alternative, and no half-baked Council is needed to placate them.

The real purpose of the Council is to provide a fig-leaf for the Dublin Government which enables them to represent Sunningdale as an anti-Partitionist victory, and a step towards a united Ireland.

Northern Ireland was paralysed by the strike, which affected power, petrol supplies and all aspects of the everyday life of the province. Unionist members of the Assembly began deserting what they saw as a sinking ship, led by Roy Bradford, who had been expressing an interest in Irish reunification shortly before, but was affected by the moral cowardice that is all too common among unionist politicians. Wilson continued to hesitate. The British Army had settled by this date on a fixed policy of not fighting on two fronts in Northern Ireland: it would concentrate on the IRA and the nationalists, so ensuring the neutrality if not the cooperation of the loyalist paramilitaries. The army too hesitated. The Ulster Defence Regiment, although a regiment of the army, was a doubtful force in the circumstances. It had been brought into being to replace the special constabulary, and was recruited from the loyalist population. Its membership overlapped considerably with the UDA. The RUC was likely to be more reliable but had never been seriously tried in a confrontation with loyalist subversion. While they all hesitated, the Executive collapsed, and Wilson underlined his weakness by going on network television and offering futile insults to the strike leaders.

Two more unsuccessful attempts were made to set up assemblies in Northern Ireland, while politics, released from the Partitionist/anti-Partitionist straitjacket of fifty years, developed to give expression to the wide variety of interests and opinions in the province, with new parties forming and many of them fading away within a few years. The acute crisis of Northern Ireland had passed by 1975: a Catholic uprising, the end of Ulster home rule, and a Protestant uprising. Unsteadily, the death-rate from political violence declined thereafter. Dublin and London negotiated, very much aware that the negotiation was now within the context of a slowly unifying Europe in which the powers and significance of national sovereignty were diminishing, equally slowly perhaps, but surely.

In 1972 and again in 1974–75, British governments (Conservative and Labour) had negotiated directly with the Provisional IRA, just as the British had negotiated in 1921. But there was a profound difference. In 1921 they negotiated with representatives of Dáil Éireann, an assembly openly elected after making its political position clear. The Provisional IRA undoubtedly represented something in Northern Ireland. But its political wing, Sinn Féin, was out-voted by the SDLP within Northern Ireland, and Sinn Féin and the SDLP together were greatly out-voted by the unionist parties. It had no mandate to speak for the people of Northern Ireland. Still less did it have a mandate to speak for the people of Ireland as a whole, since the electorate of the Republic had been choosing parliaments and governments for many decades and had never chosen Sinn Féin. Therefore it lacked a basis for negotiation. It also lacked a programme and a policy, although – *after* going into action in 1970 – it made a number of attempts to cobble these together. It belonged essentially to a different sphere of polical activity from that of programmes, policies, elections and parliaments. It was the voice of alienation: straightforward rebellion.

Anglo-Irish dealings between the two sovereign governments gradually took over the process. The British government had short-term aims: to persuade the Irish government to join more and more effectively in suppressing the IRA, to diminish violence to manageable levels in Northern Ireland and to exercise control over the loyalists, letting them know that Britain – not Paisley, Faulkner, Craig or Tyrie – ruled in the province. The Irish government had longer term objectives: to persuade the British government into suppressing the unionists with a view to an ultimate all-Ireland arrangement of some kind. The British decided to begin treating the IRA as ordinary criminals, and withdrew the special status which they had been granted in the days of internment without trial. This led to a prolonged conflict, at times bizarre, at times tragic, in which the main effort of the members of the IRA was directed towards establishing their own status as soldiers of a liberation army.

'Special Category' status for IRA prisoners was withdrawn in 1976. It had included the right of the prisoners to wear their own clothes. Now the republican prisoners (some INLA included) refused to wear prison clothes and were left naked in their cells. There began, as the conflict got out of hand in the prisons (including the women's prison in Armagh), what came to be known as the 'dirty protest', with prisoners, whose only covering was prison blankets, living in their own filth in their cells, smearing the walls with their excrement. This was a quite extraordinary protest. Prisoners are extremely limited in their means of asserting their rights; republican prisoners in Northern Ireland jails more than most, because they are commonly guarded by loyalists who despise and humiliate them. To maintain morale in such circumstances prisoners usually cultivate everything that will support their self-respect. But the republican prisoners in the late 1970s appeared to do quite the opposite.

Then, when this failed, they moved on to the ultimate prisoners' weapon – well tried in 1920 and 1921 and in a few cases earlier in the 1970s – the hunger strike. This was attempted at the end of 1980, but the strike ended in much confusion, with an agreement

143

between the prisoners and the government which was differently interpreted after the event by the two parties. In 1981 the issue was joined in the hunger strike led by a remarkable character, Bobby Sands, who died on 5 May. Nine others died after him before the strike was called off. Mrs Thatcher showed her mettle by refusing to yield an inch while the strike went on, in spite of appeals from all quarters to make some compromise. The prisoners, after all, were in reality special category prisoners, since, apart from the distinctive nature of their offences, they had not been tried or dealt with by the normal processes of the criminal law. At the end of the hunger strike the political prisoners were in fact granted much of what they had demanded. During the strike Sinn Féin found that public opinion, both in the Republic and in the North, was so moved that they were able to make electoral advances.

This inspired a diversion, at first insignificant, later to become much more marked, of republican policy from reliance on force towards participation in the politics of canvassing votes. At the Sinn Féin annual conference in 1981, Danny Morrison asked support for a policy of 'a ballot box paper in one hand and an Armalite in the other'. This has been misinterpreted. He was not urging the Armalite on the conference; he was urging the ballot. The Sinn Féin people already fully supported guns and bombs, but they regarded with deep suspicion any suggestion of participation in the parliamentary politics of the imperial enemy, Britain, or of the partition states, Northern Ireland and the Republic.

Sinn Féin in fact at this time came into serious competition with the SDLP in Northern nationalist politics, winning about 40 per cent of the nationalist vote in elections. It had a brief flash of electoral success in the Republic – with a much tinier percentage of the overall vote, concentrated in the Border counties – but subsequently fell back to about 1–2 per cent of the vote in the South. The party had become, by the 1980s, as had the IRA, overwhelmingly Northern led and Northern based.

Almost all the schemes devised by the British government for Northern Ireland, from Sunningdale to Hillsborough, would seem to have been based on behaviour theory. They provided elaborate systems (like mazes for laboratory rats) by which the people of Northern Ireland, through good or correct behaviour, would be given the incentive of more and more responsibility in their own affairs. Correct responses would be met with 'reinforcers', incorrect responses by punishment. This applied both to the Sunningdale Executive and to such concepts as 'rolling devolution'. It is as if the Whitehall civil servants and parliamentary draughtsmen who devised these schemes saw themselves as benign but strict nannies coping with unruly children (in particular the unionists) and laying down the old Victorian nursery rule that 'little birds must in their nest agree'.

The unionists of the province had learnt one lesson from the upheaval at the end of the 1960s. It was that a single-party system was unnecessary. So long as those who supported the Union could agree among themselves to give that issue all necessary priority, they could form separate parties and disagree on as many other matters as they wished. And one of the earliest reforms introduced had been electoral: the restoration in Northern Ireland (except in British general elections) of proportional representation by means of the single transferable vote. Unionist pluralism was possible without the constant risk of splitting the vote that supported the Union and letting in an anti-partitionist candidate.

Oddly enough no strong labour or socialist party emerged from this loosening in unionism, which seems to have settled down, after a winnowing out, to be represented by three parties: what is in effect the old Unionist Party, led by James Molyneux, commanding the largest share of the unionist vote; the populist and loyalist Democratic Unionist Party, led by Ian Paisley; and the Alliance Party, with the smallest share of the vote. The Alliance Party in a way is the most strictly unionist of the three, since its emphasis is on the solid benefits of the Union rather than on the ancient hostilities within the province. It was founded as a party which Protestants and Catholics could equally readily join; it is essentially a party for the professional middle classes and for residents of the more comfortable suburbs – which is why it holds a small and localized, but steady, share of unionist support.

On the nationalist side, the Social Democratic and Labour Party, which emerged at an early stage of the 'Troubles', has maintained a strong position largely through the able leadership of John Hume, who succeeded Gerry Fitt in November 1979, and through his gift

– which was also de Valera's – of diplomacy: he is a most able negotiator and played a major part both in bringing about the New Ireland Forum and in preparing the way for the Hillsborough treaty. Sinn Féin is the counterpart of the DUP – a populist party that speaks for the underclass and the alienated. Its support for and close connection with the Provisional IRA does little harm to its appeal to extreme nationalists or to the deprived, but almost certainly acts to limit its steady support to a third or less of the Catholics of Northern Ireland. In the Republic it has only the most marginal steady support.

The effects of direct rule, however, and in particular of the Hillsborough Agreement, have been to force all these parties, more and more, to try to find some way of reconciling the apparently irreconcileable in Northern Ireland. Hillsborough put severe pressure on the unionists of all stamps. They were, understandably, affronted at a treaty negotiated without consulting them although it was to concern the administration of the province and people that elected them as representatives. A unionist coalition was formed to present a united front against the Agreement and to ensure a common policy in opposition to it. A Task Force prepared a report (written by Frank Millar, then general secretary of the Official Unionist Party, Harold McCusker of the OUP and Peter Robinson, Deputy Leader of the DUP), attempting to assess the consequences of the developments of the past twenty years; but the report was not generally accepted by unionists.

But, as Robin Wilson argued in the Belfast magazine, *Fortnight*, for November 1987, the 'received wisdom' that there are two irreconcileable political traditions in the North may be somewhat superficial.

It was this received wisdom which formed the basis for the Anglo-Irish Agreement: entrenched in their opposing camps, 'the two communities' could find no other means of mutual political expression than through the surrogacy of 'the two sovereign governments' to which they defiantly held their allegiance . . . A less superficial reading of the political culture of Northern Ireland indicates a more complex underlying reality. For a start, there are four – not two – broad strands to that

146

culture. And opinion polls conducted during the 'Troubles', whose results show considerable consistency, give a fairly reliable picture of their respective weights.

*First, and this is the more popular Protestant affiliation, there is the desire for integration with Britain . . .

*Second in that community comes devolution, with a small but growing majority within that in favour of a form of devolution which entails accommodation with Catholic representatives, rather than majority rule. Such was the position taken by the Task Force report – a perspective adopted after a widespread trawl of Protestant opinion.

*This stance is paralleled amongst a majority in the Catholic community who favour participation in a structurally reformed Northern Ireland state.

*Finally, there is the 'traditional' republican alternative – though one very much revamped under the tutelage of the Adams leadership – whose support now closely matches the electoral showing of Sinn Féin.

What has happened in the late 1980s is that the British government has withdrawn its backing from Ulster unionism's former extreme position, while the right of the Irish government to interest itself in the welfare of the nationalists of Northern Ireland has been recognized. A consensus has been slowly emerging within the province, centred on a large section of the Catholic population and a large section of the Protestant population in which there is a desire for mutual agreement to make a new Northern Ireland work.

In an interview that he gave to Frank Millar (who left his job with the Unionist Party to become a journalist) for the *Irish Times* of 20 March 1989, Peter Robinson summed up his views. They are of considerable interest, since he is both thoughtful and articulate and is increasingly influential. He said:

I think the key unionist agenda must be a recognition, first, that the problem we face exists in Northern Ireland in the relationship between the two communities in Northern Ireland. Therefore, the first essential is that we decide how we can live together in Northern Ireland and how we can have structures which will

147

order our society, how we can have institutions which we can all respect and which we can all identify with.

Maybe it is easier for me to look through the other end of the telescope and indicate to you that, in the far distance, what I want in Northern Ireland is a province that is at peace, a province which has the kind of constitutional stability so that changes in elections will not cause the fall of the political structures; with constitutional arrangements that will allow the people to identify with the process and therefore rail against anybody who attacks those structures . . .

Later he said:

I think where I differ from John Hume's agenda is in the priority in how matters have to be dealt with. John Hume says that the first step that unionists must work out is their relationship with the Prime Minister of the Irish Republic so that they can agree how we share this island. I say on my agenda that the first priority is to work out how we live together in Northern Ireland; once we have done that, then we work out our relationship with the Republic of Ireland, and we can work out the relationship that the new structures that we agree on will have with the rest of the United Kingdom . . . Unionists want to be friends with the Irish Republic, but they do not want to be part of that family, and that is the distinction . . .

It is plain that there is widespread dissatisfaction with the present situation and the present arrangements in Northern Ireland – dissatisfaction is too mild a word to express what some people feel. It is in many ways absurd that so much killing and maiming should have occurred among people who have so much, politically, culturally, socially, in common. As Edna Longley put it (also in *Fortnight* for November 1987):

. . . The literature produced by Ulster people suggests that, instead of brooding on Celtic and Orange dawns, its inhabitants might accept this province-in-two-contexts as a cultural corridor. Unionists want to block the corridor at one end, republicans at the other. Culture, like common sense, insists it can't be done. Ulster Irishness and Ulster Britishness are bound to each other and to Britain and Ireland. And the Republic will have to come cleaner about its own *de facto* connections with Britain. Only by promoting circulation within and through Ulster will the place ever be part of a healthy system.

The Border is open; it is easy to cross. What Ms Longley suggests is the easiest thing in the world to do, and people who desired a united Ireland might have done well long ago to cross not only the Border but several other invisible lines, to listen as well as to preach. But new structures are now needed. Hillsborough appears to be serving its purpose of forcing the necessary rethinking. There are three distinct problems involved in the Northern 'Troubles', and it is most important to keep the distinction clear, although of course all three interact. The three concern the question of the Union with Britain, the question of the unification of Ireland, and the question of the relationship between the two main politico-religious groupings within Northern Ireland itself.

Northern nationalists are believed to favour the unification of Ireland, while northern loyalists are believed to favour the Union with Britain. But in practice, in everyday life, Northern nationalists often react to the South much as Northern unionists do. Ulster is different, and seventy years of separation of systems has given Northern Ireland an even more markedly different character. And Northern loyalists often react to the English much as Northern nationalists do. British actions or decisions are frequently resented, in particular when they curb the independence or ignore the stated wishes of Ulster people. There is a strong negative element in both nationalism and loyalism in the North. Nationalists resent, not so much British rule as such but unionist rule with British backing. They look to the South with somewhat mixed feelings. Loyalists are not so much attached to the political connection to Britain (the cultural connection they probably value more) as determined not to be brought under Dublin rule.

It is possible to reconcile these conflicting aspirations and positions, through a compromise that would involve a new constitution for Northern Ireland: a devolution that would create a self-governing state, much more like the Irish Free State of 1922–1937 than the Northern Ireland of 1920–1972, or perhaps, more drastically, constitutionally more like the Canada of today.

It is fairly well agreed among the great majority of people of all parties, and recognized by the British and Irish governments, that whatever permanent arrangements are made for (and by) Northern Ireland they should serve certain purposes. These include bringing together in a common union people who, up to now, have failed to agree on their allegiance; ensuring equality under law; providing for the internal tranquility of the State and its external defence; securing the personal and civil rights and liberties of all citizens; promoting the general welfare; and providing recognition for the different political and cultural traditions and aspirations within the State.

This is not to suggest UDI, or any unilateral action. Mr Robinson was right, in his *Irish Times* interview, in saying that the prime problem is 'how we live together in Northern Ireland'. But he was wrong in saying that this must be addressed first, Northern Ireland's external relations second. For the problem of the internal relations in Northern Ireland arises from the problem of its external relations. It is precisely the question of how to relate to Britain on the one hand, to the Republic on the other, that causes the internal problem. Therefore neither can usefully be given priority over the other in the negotiations that must now, sooner or later, be undertaken. The governments of the Republic and of Great Britain together with all the Northern Ireland parties – including Sinn Féin and the DUP – must ultimately be involved in whatever settlement it is possible to achieve. The DUP has shown a reasonably open-minded willingness to meet with other groups and discuss possible future arrangements for the province. But it has shirked responsibility. It has evaded substantive discussions leading to governmental decisions of consequence, obviously fearful of the stale old Ulster cry of 'Lundy!', of being accused, when any compromise is made, of selling the pass.

And the exclusion of parties who have not renounced violence is humbug. Pacifism is not a tenet of any party or government seriously involved. If old institutions are to be scrapped – as they should be – it is pointless to ask people such as the Provisional IRA to respect them. If the 'men of violence' are being asked to respect new institutions, then: they should be asked. The renunciation of violence, too, must be negotiated. And if the paramilitary organiz- ations on both sides are to be persuaded to lay down their arms and honour a new constitution for Northern Ireland, then the final settlement should include an amnesty. This would involve releasing a few violent criminals, for such people are attracted to paramilitary organizations, just as they are attracted to mercenary armies and 'special forces' such as the British SAS or the American Green Berets. But, as Cardinal Ó Fiaich pointed out at the time of the Long Kesh hunger strike of 1981, most IRA volunteers are not criminals in the ordinary sense, horrific though some of the effects of their deeds may be.

The British insistence on giving priority to 'the defeat of terrorism' takes an easy option, but one that leaves problems unsolved. It is easy for them, since, apart from striking rarely in Great Britain, 'terrorism' is for the most part something happening in what, for most British people in their hearts, is another country. (This is why the terrorists occasionally have tried to strike savagely at the heart of British rule, at Airey Neave, at Lord Mountbatten, at the Prime Minister and her government). Terrorism must indeed be defeated. But not by shooting suspects dead at checkpoints, by SAS assassinations, by beatings in police cells, by midnight searches of working-class homes, by the testimony of perjurers in Diplock courts presided over by deeply prejudiced judges. Rather it must be defeated by depriving the terrorists of their support, which means making life tolerable for all in Northern Ireland. While most people there live, mostly, reasonably normal lives, there are pockets and patches where whole communities have endured now for almost twenty years constant and ever-present cruel oppression, tolerating the tyranny of their paramilitary 'defenders' because those defenders attack the hated military and paramilitary-police presence in their midst.

But all, even of the normal lives, have been touched by the 'Troubles' by now. Everyone knows someone or has some relation who has been killed or maimed. Everyone has experienced at some stage the presence of violent death or the threat of it. There is much bitterness. But there is also a fairly widespread feeling of regret –

remorse, even – for past failings. And a new realism, forced on the people of Northern Ireland and on the people of the Republic, which compels compromise. What is necessary, and what has not been forthcoming, is acknowledgment by the British government too that it has been at fault and that it must make decisions some of which may be hurtful to British pride.

One of the central difficulties of the problem lies in the fact that it is not essentially a local problem, but a general problem made acute by special local emphases. It is a British problem. It is a problem of the whole developed Western world. The decline of certain kinds of heavy industry has afflicted Scotland and northern England, as well as Northern Ireland, with a variety of social ills. British society too has become quite violent in the years since the Second World War, but the violence on the whole has no clear political focus. The anger of the effectively disenfranchised poor is directed, like that of the Byzantine mob or the Irish peasants of the nineteenth century, into faction fighting, into 'soccer violence' and crime.

Political decisions are certainly necessary in Ireland, and the only ones that will work are such as will let people know that, in reasonable measure, they have control of their own destinies. What people know now (not only in Northern Ireland) is that their lives are profoundly affected by the actions of remote persons, in distant bureaucracies, or manipulating the stock exchanges in London, New York or Tokyo.

The desire for decentralization was a significant element in the reactive nationalisms that strove against the Procrustean constraints of the early modern nation-states. The nation-states in question are now obsolescent, and the economies that sustained them obsolete or extinct. We have entered an age of universal states, like the USA, the USSR and the nascent European Community. The USA is somewhat exceptional among these, since it may be regarded in many ways as simply a gigantic nation-state, embracing several very large nations (one of which, the South, rose in an unsuccessful reactive-nationalist rebellion in the middle of the last century), that have been bonded together by an extraordinarily powerful social pressure to conformity. And even these universal states are finding it necessary to defer to a new world economy – which is in itself highly unbalanced. The end of the Cold War (if it has ended) may well be related to the sudden realization by all of the industrialized parts of the world, including the USA, the USSR and Europe, that they enjoy affluence, or comparative affluence, at the expense of the Third World. They have interests in common.

Whatever is to happen in Ireland must happen within this context. Ireland is small, and its people can have little or no say in the dangerous speculations by which entrepreneurs in Wall Street and elsewhere make fortunes from the accumulation of debt rather than the accumulation of equity, from shuffling money rather than producing goods – although the activities on Wall Street and in other such centres (including notably the City of London) have profound effects on their daily lives. Mass unemployment is one of the products of the policies that have been pursued in London, Washington and elsewhere for many years now. And unemployment paralyses both societies in Ireland, that of Northern Ireland and that of the Republic. This is a major economic problem common to the whole island. For Ireland to be a good country to live in again the problem must be solved.

The promotion and fostering of new industry is not the answer, or at least not the whole answer. This has been, up to a point, a standard practice of present-day governments in their attempts to increase national production and productivity. Insofar as the practice claims to address the needs of the unemployed it is at best contradictory. For the creation of unemployment is a necessary and deliberate part of the neo-conservative policies now in force through much of the Western world. Contemporary techniques of manufacture and production require less and less labour; and less and less do they require the kind of craft skills that once gave a reasonable bargaining position to labour. Contemporary neo-conservatism aims at the creation of affluent élites enjoying the products of largely cybernetic production systems, waited on by serfs in 'service industries' and holding at bay both what they have learned to call 'the underclass' and that very large underclass commonly called 'the Third World'. Disraeli's 'two nations' may be observed today throughout North America and Britain. And, as well as the other much discussed two nations, Disraeli's two nations are present in Northern Ireland (and the Republic). This is to say that the Irish crisis of the past twenty years cannot be treated in isolation.

The particular Ulster problem is political, not economic or religious; but it involves economics and religion. A solution of the political problem would do no more than clear the way for tackling other problems. But it must be found.

The political problem is most commonly presented in terms of two mutually antagonistic aspirations: the maintenance of the Union (in its extreme form, by full integration of Northern Ireland into the United Kingdom); and an independent all-Ireland republic. As was pointed out at the very beginning of this book, and as should be clear from any serious study of the subject, neither is a practical option. No political purpose would be served by forcing a solution that would be violently opposed and that would perpetuate grievances.

'Devolution' is the preferred unionist alternative to integration. But the devolution of 1920 must be regarded as a failed experiment. A revival of the old Stormont is simply not acceptable to a very large part of the population of Northern Ireland. Withdrawal of the British from the province, combined with a permanent guarantee of the Border (by both Dublin and London) is an option that has not been sufficiently considered.

This solution has been avoided in most discussion, on the grounds that it would lead to a 'blood-bath'. The fear is not unreasonable, but it is misplaced. An attempt to force Northern Ireland into the Republic would certainly provoke violence, much greater than has been seen so far, and would furthermore be pointless, since it would merely lead to major problems for the indefinite future. But the creation, with the financial and moral help of the London and Dublin governments, of a third State within the British Isles, connected perhaps to Britain through the Crown and to the Republic through close and intimate treaty relations, is far from impossible. Hillsborough, in fact, for all its arbitrariness, has made it much easier.

British governments, in particular over the twenty years of trouble, have shown a strong inclination to suppress discussion of the possibility of independence for Northern Ireland. This lends support to the view that the question of British prestige is quite central to the problem of Northern Ireland. Although British governments, like most of the British people, surely feel strong inclinations at times to rid themselves of the problems, such inclinations must contend with a reluctance to let go – and to admit, finally, that they cannot govern Ireland. And the Queen, in the 1970s, at the time when Welsh and Scottish nationalisms were actively agitating, expressed understandable dismay at the possibility that 'her United Kingdom' might be broken up.

Within Northern Ireland, only one group has fairly consistently pursued the independence option – the UDA. And the UDA is not respectable. But, then, the whole problem is not very respectable. It is an option that deserves very serious consideration. While it is not what most people involved want, it may be the only option that most people involved, in the long run, would be prepared to accept with a good grace.

As things stand, therefore, a substantial move towards independence seems unlikely. But things can change quite quickly, especially as there has been for the past few years a kind of stalemate in the affairs of the province. Any such move must be begun either by the two governments concerned or by some form of popular initiative. Negotiations between Dublin and London and representatives of the people of Northern Ireland would be necessary. A referendum or plebiscite is not desirable: these are wholly open to manipulation by the government or bureaucracy that devises the wording of the questions to be put. An election of representatives to negotiate, on the other hand, is in conformity with the style of free government established in the Irish and British tradition.

There exists in all parts of Ireland a humanity in personal and community relations which is belied by the horrors of the 'Troubles'. There was a time, for all of the nineteenth century and the early part of the twentieth, when Ireland as a whole was as ungovernable as Northern Ireland is now. But after the bloodshed and disorder associated with the winning of independence, the new Irish State settled down to be a peaceful and crime-free place, where people felt individually free and also, poor or rich, thought of themselves as valued and honoured citizens of a state that admitted its responsibility to them. The responsibility was poorly discharged, but for several decades not because of ill-will but because of failures and inadequacies of policy. People in government tried. And people built industries and services, conscious that they were working for

155

their nation as well as for themselves. The failures have continued. So have the achievements. The sense of community, that was powerful in the 1930s and 1940s, has diminished largely because of the turning of so much of the country's leadership to the jungle laws of neo-conservative capitalism. But Ireland, even if it did not have time or scope to achieve the justice, balance and reasonableness of Scandinavian societies, at least showed for some decades that it could steer a course between the state centralism of the East and the cruel money-worshipping ideologies of the West. The experiment of Irish independence has only begun. It is time to extend it to Northern Ireland.

It is objected that Northern Ireland is too small to survive economically on its own. This is an objection without substance. Nowadays, not even the largest state survives economically on its own. Many independent states are smaller than Northern Ireland and the Republic is, in population terms, only twice as big. Given a measure of wisdom and tolerance among its people, Northern Ireland could be a viable small state. At present its infrastructure and social services are supported with the help of a very considerable subvention from Great Britain. Were Northern Ireland to become politically independent, it would obviously be necessary for the United Kingdom, as part of its contribution to the solution of a problem for which Britain has direct responsibility, to phase out these subventions gradually.

We all have to face the great social difficulties being created by 'post-industrialism', and to be prepared to devise a new politics. A new social democracy is needed. There has been much crowing in the Western press recently over the 'failure of socialism' in the East. What has failed in fact is state centralism. It is a very blinkered vision that sees America and Britain as instances of the 'success' of capitalism. But such a blinkered view we are regularly offered. Yet Sweden, under socialist government for many years, is – by purely capitalist measures – narrowly more successful than the United States of America. And if we use a humanist measure, Sweden is by a very wide margin the superior of the two. All Ireland has to cope with these questions in the immediate future. No solution of the 'Ulster problem' will relieve the country of these other problems. But the conflict that has gone on for twenty years must end first.

Since the abolition of Stormont the various attempts made by British governments to offer a solution have had a flaw that vitiated their purpose. The British recognized that the Ulster problem was one to be solved within that province, and they recognized the 'Irish dimension'; yet the solutions proposed involved a strengthening of British control – even if this, at each stage, was intended to be no more than temporary. The Sunningdale arrangement, for example, with its Assembly, Executive and power-sharing, was no more than the shadow of parliamentary democracy. Power-sharing, it could well be argued, wasn't even that, since it contravened some generally accepted principles of the parliamentary democratic system. The fatal flaw was that politicians in Northern Ireland were being offered some of the trappings of power but none of the reality. Power has remained since 1972 in the hands of the Secretary of State for Northern Ireland and of the British army (which has displayed some capacity for independence of action or inaction).

One of the excuses offered for this, and one of the chief objections to an independent Northern Ireland, concerns the majority-minority relationship within the province. Any new constitution for Northern Ireland would have to be worked out with the consent and collaboration of the two sovereign governments at present concerned, those of the United Kingdom and of the Republic, but on the basis that these two governments should support an agreement arrived at by the parties in Northern Ireland, rather than imposing their own solution. The primary requirement then is the constitution upon which the people of Northern Ireland might agree for themselves; the secondary is the consequent arrangements that must be made with the other two governments. Since these secondary arrangements are bound to include guarantees – for the autonomy of the new state and for the full protection of minorities within it – they should be incorporated in the new constitution much as the Anglo-Irish Treaty of 1921 was incorporated in the Constitution of the Irish Free State.

De jure recognition of the new Ulster state should be given by both governments; while the intimate relations that have long existed between the peoples of the whole archipelago might perhaps be recognized by a declaration (similar to the declaration in the

Ireland Act 1949) that the citizens of any of the three states shall not be regarded as foreigners in any of the others.

One of the objections to such a solution arises from the fear of Catholic nationalists in the North that, in an independent Northern Ireland, they would be subject to oppression from a new Stormont now freed from British restraint. This is to misread how the old Stormont functioned. Sixty per cent of the population could only oppress 40 per cent with British backing and consent. Stormont had the police; Britain had the army. Without the British army, and in the face of guarantees by Ireland and the United Kingdom, the unionists simply could not oppress the nationalists without bringing their province into chaos and ruin. And it is most unlikely – given that the danger of a Dublin takeover was removed – that they would wish to do so.

If we look to the future we must bear in mind that changes are now occurring in the world whose consequences – even in the short term – are unpredictable. European union – which may lead to President Gorbachev's 'European Home', including the East – is, dimly, perhaps, within sight, but what form it may take no one can say. But it is obvious that, for the sake of all Ireland, North and South, and of Britain, and of Europe, the unnecessary conflict in Northern Ireland must end soon. There was a moment, in late 1987, when the whole island listened to Gordon Wilson describing in a radio interview how his dying daughter, Marie, a student nurse in the Royal Victoria Hospital in Belfast, had spoken to him as they both lay buried under rubble from the bomb that had exploded just before a Remembrance Day parade in Enniskillen, killing eleven people who were simply waiting for the ceremony to begin. He forgave and prayed for those who planted the bomb. His is the justice that will in the end prevail.

Writing as a citizen of the Republic, I would like to see an independent united Ireland and would welcome all the people of Northern Ireland as fellow citizens. But only if that were what they wished; and it is plainly not. And – we are speaking of administrations, tax systems, jurisdictions – it is not, in itself, all that important. What is perhaps important is the question of the monarchy. There is a significant difference between being a citizen of a republic and being the subject of a monarch. The example of the Scandinavian countries shows that it is possible to have monarchies that preside ceremonially and comparatively harmlessly over states that are in many respects republics. But Britain is not quite like that: it maintains throughout its social and political system the whole apparatus of deference and social class. The question, however, can probably be safely left to the future.

Meantime, the Border is open, and I wish my brothers and sisters in the North – all of them – well.

11

Chronology of Events

1610	Beginning of the Plantation of Ulster.
1801	Formation of the United Kingdom of Great Britain and Ireland.
1829	Catholic Emancipation.
1869	Church Disestablishment Act for Ireland.
1886	First Home Rule Bill.
1893	Second Home Rule Bill.
1912	Third Home Rule Bill.
1913	Formation of Ulster Volunteer Force, Irish National Volunteers and Irish Citizen Army.
1914	Beginning of Great War.
	Passage and suspension of third Home Rule Bill (Government of Ireland Act 1914).
1916	Easter Rising, in Dublin and elsewhere.
	Very heavy Irish casualties in the opening of the Battle of the Somme.
1918	End of the Great War.
	Sinn Féin victorious in Ireland in general election.
1919	First meeting of Dáil Éireann in Dublin. Armed resistance to British rule begins.
1920	Government of Ireland Act 1920 enacts Partition.
1921	First meeting of Parliament of Northern Ireland.
	Anglo-Irish Treaty signed.
1922	Dáil Éireann narrowly ratifies the Treaty.
	Beginning of the Irish Free State.
	Civil War begins.
	232 people killed in violence in Northern Ireland.
1923	Defeat of Republicans in civil war.
1925	The Border ratified by Irish Free State Government.

1932	Éamon de Valera leads Fianna Fáil party to victory in election in the Irish Free State.
1937	De Valera sponsors new Constitution in the Irish Free State, now named 'Ireland'.
1939–1945	Irish State neutral in Second World War.
1948	Irish State declares a Republic.
1949	The British 'Ireland Act 1949' guarantees status of Northern Ireland.
1965	Seán Lemass, Taoiseach of the Republic, meets Terence O'Neill, Prime Minister of Northern Ireland.
1967	Foundation of Northern Ireland Civil Rights Association.
1968	Bloodshed begins at civil rights march in Derry.
1969	Resignation of O'Neill.
	Violence in Derry and Belfast leads to deployment of British Army on streets of Northern Ireland.
	IRA splits into Official IRA and Provisional IRA.
1970	Ulster Defence Regiment established.
	Conservatives (Edward Heath) defeat Labour government (Harold Wilson) in British election.
	British Army curfew in the Falls area of Belfast leads to severe violence.
	SDLP formed.
	Ian Paisley elected to Stormont as MP for North Antrim.
1971	Brian Faulkner becomes PM of Northern Ireland.
	SDLP withdraws from Stormont.
	Internment without trial introduced.
	Widespread and extreme violence.
1972	Bloody Sunday: British Parachute Regiment shoots dead 13 unarmed young men and youths at civil rights demonstration in Derry.
	British Embassy in Dublin burned.
	Official IRA kills seven (mostly cleaning women) with bomb in Aldershot Barracks.
	Stormont suspended: direct British rule in Northern Ireland.
	Official IRA call ceasefire.

Provisional IRA-British truce made and broken.

'Bloody Friday': Provisional IRA kill 9 people with 22 bombs in Belfast.

Provisional IRA kill 8 people with bomb in Claudy.

Freelance British agents kill 2 people with bomb in Dublin.

1973   Ireland and the United Kingdom become members of the EEC.

Jack Lynch (Fianna Fáil) defeated in election by Fine Gael and Labour: coalition government in Republic headed by Liam Cosgrave.

New assembly set up in Northern Ireland.

Conference of Irish and British ministers and Northern Ireland politicians produces the Sunningdale Agreement, for a power-sharing Executive in Northern Ireland and for a Council of Ireland.

1974   Unionist Party splits.

Labour (Harold Wilson) defeats the Conservative Government (Edward Heath) in two British elections.

UWC strike paralyses Northern Ireland and brings down the Executive.

UDA bombs in the Republic kill 30 people.

1975   Constitutional Convention set up in Northern Ireland.

1976   5 Catholics and 10 Protestants killed in South Armagh murders on 4 and 5 January.

SAS moves into South Armagh.

British Ambassador assassinated in Dublin.

1977   Fianna Fáil (Jack Lynch) defeats coalition government in Republic.

1978   'Dirty Protest' in Maze Prison, Long Kesh.

1979   Assassination of Airey Neave, Conservative spokesman on Northern Ireland, in the House of Commons.

Conservatives (Margaret Thatcher) defeat Labour (James Callaghan) in British election.

18 British soldiers killed in Provisional IRA ambush near Warrenpoint.

Earl Mountbatten killed by Provisional IRA bomb on his boat in Sligo Bay.

	Jack Lynch succeeded by Charles Haughey as leader of Fianna Fáil and Taoiseach.
1980	Hunger strike begun in Maze Prison; then called off.
1981	Hunger strike in Maze Prison, Long Kesh, leads to death of 10 Republican prisoners before it is called off. Fine Gael and Labour defeat Fianna Fáil (Charles Haughey) and form coalition government (Garret FitzGerald) in the Republic.
1982	Fianna Fáil defeats Coalition government in election in the Republic. Great Britain, with American help, defeats Argentina in war in the South Atlantic. New Northern Ireland Assembly Act passed in Britain. Assembly elected. Fine Gael and Labour (FitzGerald) defeat Fianna Fáil (Haughey) in election in the Republic.
1983	'New Ireland Forum' meets in Dublin. Conservatives (Margaret Thatcher) win British election. 15 of 17 Westminster seats won by unionists from Northern Ireland, one by SDLP and one by SF.
1984	New Ireland Forum publishes report. Ian Paisley, John Hume and John Taylor returned from Northern Ireland in elections for European Parliament. Margaret Thatcher escapes in Provisional IRA attempt to kill members of the British Cabinet by bombing their hotel during Conservative conference in Brighton. Margaret Thatcher rejects the Forum report.
1985	Anglo-Irish treaty signed at Hillsborough, Co. Down.
1986	In a cover-up of RUC 'shoot-to-kill' activities, John Stalker is removed from an inquiry into that force.
1987	Fianna Fáil (Charles Haughey) defeats the Coalition government in election in the Republic.

12

Some Organizations

DUP	Democratic Unionist Party.
EEC	European Economic Community.
FF	Fianna Fáil (largest political party in the Republic).
FG	Fine Gael (second party in the Republic).
ILP	Irish Labour Party.
INLA	Irish National Liberation Army.
IRA	Irish Republican Army.
IRSP	Irish Republican Socialist Party.
NICRA	Northern Ireland Civil Rights Association.
OIRA	Official Irish Republican Army.
OUP	Official Unionist Party.
PD	Progressive Democratic Party.
PIRA	Provisional Irish Republican Army.
RUC	Royal Ulster Constabulary.
SF	Sinn Féin.
SDLP	Social Democratic and Labour Party.
UDA	Ulster Defence Association.
UDR	Ulster Defence Regiment.
UVF	Ulster Volunteer Force.
UWC	Ulster Workers' Council.
WP	Workers' Party.

13

Select Bibliography

This book is not a history of the 'Troubles' in Northern Ireland, but an essay, a discussion of where we are and where we go from here. I have avoided footnotes and incorporated such few textual references as were necessary in the text.

The history has been more than adequately dealt with in the past twenty years by numerous writers. The list of works is by now extremely large, and I offer here only a short selection of them. The reader with a serious interest in this problem is strongly recommended to consult the Linenhall Library in Belfast, which has by far the best collection of materials relating to the question.

As I have been expressing personal opinions in this work, I begin by offering the reader a short list of earlier works of my own in which she or he may find some backing for the views here expressed (as well as some evidence for changing opinion).

L. de Paor, *Divided Ulster* (Harmondsworth 1970).
'The Rebel Mind: Republican and Loyalist', in Richard Kearney, ed., *The Irish Mind* (Dublin 1985), pp. 157–187.
The Peoples of Ireland from Prehistory to Modern Times (London 1986).
Paul Arthur, *Government and Politics of Northern Ireland* (New York 1981).
J. Bowyer Bell, *The Secret Army: the I.R.A. 1916–1969* (Cambridge Mass 1980).
Paul Bew et al., *The State in Northern Ireland, 1921–1972: Political Forces and Social Classes* (Manchester 1979).

Kevin Boyle et al., *Law and State: the Case for Northern Ireland* (Amherst 1975).

Kevin Boyle et al., *Ten Years On in Northern Ireland: the Legal Control of Political Violence* (London 1980).

Patrick Buckland, *A History of Northern Ireland* (New York 1981).

Tim Pat Coogan, *On the Blanket: the H-Block Story* (London 1981).

Michael Farrell, *Northern Ireland: The Orange State* (London 1970).

Peter Gibbon, *The Origins of Ulster Unionism* (Manchester 1975).

John F. Harbinson, *The Ulster Unionist Party, 1882–1973: Its Development and Organization* (Belfast 1974).

Rosemary Harris, *Prejudice and Toleration in Ulster* (Totowa, NJ 1972).

M. R. Heslinga, *The Irish Border as a Cultural Divide* (Atlantic Highlands, NJ 1980).

F. S. L. Lyons, *Culture and Anarchy in Ireland: 1819 to 1939* (New York 1979).

Ed Moloney and Andy Pollak, *Paisley* (Dublin 1986).

Éamon McCann, *War and an Irish Town* (London 1981).

David Miller, *Queen's Rebels: a Historical Study of Ulster Loyalism* (New York 1978).

John A. Murphy, *Ireland in the Twentieth Century* (Dublin 1975).

Conor Cruise O'Brien, *States of Ireland* (London 1972).

Liam O'Dowd et al., *Northern Ireland from Civil Rights to Civil War* (Atlantic Highlands, NJ 1981).

Pádraig O'Malley, *The Uncivil Wars: Ireland Today* (Belfast 1983).

Richard Rose, *Governing Without Consensus: An Irish Perspective* (Boston MA 1971).

A. T. Q. Stewart, *The Narrow Ground: Aspects of Ulster History, 1606– 1969* (London 1977).

Files of *Fortnight, Magill,* and the *Irish Times* might also be consulted.

Index

(N) = (footnote)

INDEX

INDEX

INDEX

INDEX